TENNESSEE SOLDIERS IN THE REVOLUTION

A ROSTER OF SOLDIERS LIVING DURING THE REVOLU-
TIONARY WAR IN THE COUNTIES OF WASHINGTON
AND SULLIVAN. TAKEN FROM THE REVOLUTIONARY
ARMY ACCOUNTS OF NORTH CAROLINA

●

Compiled by

PENELOPE JOHNSON ALLEN

State Vice Regent

TENNESSEE DAUGHTERS *of the* AMERICAN REVOLUTION

Published under the Auspices of
THE TENNESSEE SOCIETY, DAUGHTERS *of the* AMERICAN
REVOLUTION, 1935
MRS. ALLEN HARRIS, *State Regent*

Originally Published 1935

SOUTHERN HISTORICAL PRESS, INC.
PO BOX 1267
Greenville, SC   29601

ISBN #978-1-63914-088-6

Printed in the United States of America

CONTENTS

PREFACE

THE following list of Revolutionary soldiers and patriots is taken from the unpublished Revolutionary Army Accounts of North Carolina which are a part of the State Archives, at Raleigh.

The compiler's thanks are due to Mr. R. B. House, Secretary of the North Carolina Historical Commission, and to Mrs. William West, Custodian of Records, for many kindnesses shown during the preparation of this work.

PENELOPE JOHNSON ALLEN.

"TOOANTUH"
CHATTANOOGA,
TENNESSEE.

October 1, 1935.

INTRODUCTION

THE Revolutionary history of Tennessee belongs to her mother state, and in the archives of North Carolina are to be found many interesting records of the valorous services performed by the men on her western frontier during the Struggle for Independence. Before the Revolutionary War began, the country west of the Allegheny Mountains, was being cleared and tended by pioneers who braved the dangers of forest and Indian to establish new homes in the beautiful valleys of what is now East Tennessee. The tide of emigration had turned westward in response to the reports of the Long Hunters of plentiful game and fertile soil.

As early as 1769, William Bean had staked his claim and built a cabin on Boon's Creek, in what is now Washington County, and very soon thereafter friends and relatives from Pittsylvania County, Virginia, from whence he came, joined him in the new country. Other settlers followed and the Watauga Association was formed.

In 1777, the territory lying west of the mountains was formed into the county of Washington.

These North Carolina frontiersmen were patriots. The same spirit of independence which moved them to face the dangers of the wilderness, turned them also against British taxes. The Indians with whom they were contending for the land whereon they were building their homes were allies of the English.

The extension of the western boundary line between North Carolina and Virginia, in 1780, threw a large settlement that had hitherto considered itself to be on Virginia soil, into the domain of North Carolina. This territory was formed into a second new county and named for General Sullivan.

The militia was organized in Washington and Sullivan Counties, after the manner of the rest of North Carolina. Companies were formed from tall gaunt men whith sharp eyes and steady fingers—bred to the rifle from childhood. But for them the fight was in both directions—English armies on the East, Indian bands on the West. Living with gun in hand they were always ready to answer the call to arms.

Ramsey, in his Annals of Tennessee, has preserved the names of a few of the men who were active in Captain William Bean's Company in 1779.

In the North Carolina Revolutionary Army Accounts (unpublished), Vol. XI, page 18, folio 2, claims dated November, 1777, are found the following items paid to men who were then living in the Watauga settlement.

"To Capt. James Holles for himself and company pay £67—£390,2,6."

"To Capt. George Russell, for pay for himself and company £77—£740,16."

P. 20, folio 2. "To Capt. James Robertson for himself and company's pay £91—2066,5,6."

"To Col. John Carter for himself and regiment £312—£166,10."

P. 20, folio 4. "To Col. John Sevier for sundry persons, for cart and horse £331—£175,5."

Vol. VIII, page 70, folio 4:

Sept., 1777, Samuel Hanley, £11-17,6

Aug., 1777, Jashu Hinder, £11,17,6

June, 1777, Samuel Looney, £11-17,6

Aug., 1777, Thomas Hughs, £11-17,6

Aug., 1777, Peter Rasor, £11,15

Aug., 1777, Michael Border, £11-15,

Aug., 1777, Philip Duttenger, £11-15,

Oct., 1777, George Wampler, £23,6

Oct., 1777, John Fain, £15,4,3

Oct., 1777, Samuel Vance, £15,0,5

Oct., 1777, William Johnston, £6.

Oct., 1777, John Gilliham, £14-17,6

Sept., 1777, Samuel Weir, £15.

Sept., 1777, George Vaught, £12-13,9

Oct., 1777, Isaac Shelby, £14,14,4

Oct., 1777, Isaac Shelby, £9,4

Oct., 1777, Thomas Little, £3,0,15

The militia of the two western counties was very active up to the close of the Revolutionary War, and for sometime thereafter in Indian campaigns. The Watauga and Holston settlers carried on a continuous struggle with the Indians. At one time a great tribal confederacy was planned by the British, which design, if carried out, would have created a formidable obstruction to the west of the colonists, extending from Canada to Florida.

An expedition against the Chickamauga Indians, in April, 1779, led by Col. Evan Shelby and Lt.-Col. Charles Robertson, destroyed this plan, and for the time being, checked the hostilities of the Indians. Five hundred men from Washington and Sullivan Counties took part in this campaign and overcame the Indians at the first Battle of Chickamauga.

In the summer of 1780, a regiment of Watauga men commanded by Col. Charles Robertson did good service in the South Carolina campaign and participated in several battles.

On October 7, 1780, the memorable Battle of King's Mountain took place, and the part played by the "over-mountain" men in defeat of General

Ferguson has been described by competent historians as the turning point in the Revolution.

Returning home from this great victory another excursion was made into the Cherokee Country under the leadership of Col. John Sevier.

A third expedition was ordered against the implacable Chickamaugas by the State of North Carolina, in the fall of 1782, and was commanded by General Joseph McDowell and Col. John Sevier. A thousand men raised in the western counties comprised the troops for this attack on the Indians who were growing increasingly hostile to the Americans as the result of the labors of British agents among them.

From the North Carolina Colonial and State Records, Vol. 16, page 450, the following extract from a letter of Governor Alexander Martin to the North Carolina delegates in Congress, dated New Bern, Nov. 2d, 1782, is taken:

"The 20th ultimo near one thousand militia marched in two divisions, under command of Brigadier General McDowell and Col. Sevier, from Morgan District, against the Chickammogy and other hostile towns of the Cherokees. This expedition was absolutely necessary and was by the advice of the Council of State, ordered out."

The state of North Carolina began enacting legislation for the payment of her soldiers and the settling of war claims in 1780. In 1781, a board of Auditors was established for the settlement of public claims, and Anthony Bledsoe, a resident of Sullivan County, was named as one of the Auditors for Salisbury district to which Washington and Sullivan Counties then belonged.

At the same time an act was passed by the General Assembly providing for the payment for military duty and other claims against the state for articles furnished or impressed. In April, 1782, an "Act for the Relief of Officers of the Continental Line" was passed, and at the same session an amendment to this act provided "that all claims now due and unsettled shall be liquidated in specie, by the district auditors under the same rules and regulations as prescribed by the before recited act." In section five of the same act the names of the auditors for the different districts of the state are given.

For Washington and Sullivan Counties—Anthony Bledsoe, Edmund Williams and Landon Carter are named.

In 1783, an Act authorizing the opening of a land office for the redemption of specie and other certificates was passed, and all soldiers holding specie or certificates were enabled to redeem them by taking land in exchange, at a rate fixed by the state.

7

John Armstrong was appointed entry taker, and the Land Office was opened at Hillsboro, in Orange County.

Soldiers from all over the state entered land in North Carolina's vast western domain, but the list which follows is confined to those soldiers who were paid by Bledsoe, Carter and Williams, indicating that they were living during the time of their active service in the counties of Washington and Sullivan. These payments began June 12, 1782, and continued until August 15, 1783.

Many names appear more than once in the account books, as frequently a man had more than one claim against the state. Other repetitions indicate different individuals of the same name. The spelling of proper names depended on the Clerk's ear and education, so the same person will sometimes appear under a pleasing variety of surnames.

Vol. 24, page 325:

1780

An act to establish a board of Auditors for the purpose of selling and adjusting the Public Accounts of the State and other purposes.

Vol. 24, page 373:

1781

An act for appointing District Auditors for the settlement of Public Claims, etc. (This act established five district boards and two for the district of Salisbury. Anthony Bledsaw is named as one of the auditors in the Salisbury board.)

Vol. 24, page 387:

Provides for the payment of military duty and other claims against the State for articles furnished or impressed.

Vol. 24, page 409:

1782

An Act for the Relief of Officers of the Continental line, etc.

Vol. 24, page 422:

General Assembly, Hillsboro, April, 1782. Alexander Martin, Governor.

"An act to amend an act, etc."

Sec. 2. Be it therefore further enacted by the General Assembly of the State of North Carolina, and it is hereby enacted, by the same, that all claims now due, and unsettled, shall be liquidated in specie, by the district auditors under the same rules and regulations, as prescribed by the before recited act.

Sec. 5. And be it further enacted by the aforesaid authority that the following persons be, and they are hereby appointed district auditors, to wit—

For Washington and Sullivan Counties—Anthony Bledsow, Edmund Williams and Landon Carter.

Vol. 24, page 478:

1783

Act for opening a land office for the redemption of specie and other certificates.

(See also Vol. 25, page 4.)

COLONEL ANTHONY BLEDSOE

COLONEL ANTHONY BLEDSOE was born in Orange County, Virginia, in 1733. He received a good education for that time and became a surveyor. In early life he removed to the western frontier, where he served as Captain in the colonial militia in 1774. He was with Col. William Christian in his expedition against the Indians in 1776. The next year, he was left by Col. Christian in command of 600 men at Long Island for protection of the frontier, and in 1778 Major Bledsoe was elected to the General Assembly, of Virginia, from Washington County, Virginia. The next year he presented a bill for the extension of the line between Virginia and North Carolina, which was passed. This placed Col. Bledsoe in North Carolina.

In 1781, North Carolina passed an act for establishing a board of Auditors to adjust Public Accounts growing out of Revolutionary war. Anthony Bledsoe was named as a member of the board for Salisbury district which served the western settlements.

With the development of the Cumberland country, Colonel Bledsoe moved his family west again, and settled in what is now Sumner County. He located a beautiful place two miles north of Bledsoe Lick calling it "Greenfield." He was a member of the first court of Davidson County when it was organized in 1783, and was elected colonel by the county militia. Col. Bledsoe was killed by Indians on the night of July 20, 1788, during an attack on the fort at Bledsoe's Lick, where he had moved his family for safety during the Indian hostilities.

Next to James Robertson, Col. Bledsoe was the most valuable member of the Cumberland settlement and his loss was a great blow.

Col. Anthony Bledsoe married, in 1760, Mary Ramsey, of Augusta County, Virginia. They were the parents of eleven children.

COLONEL LANDON CARTER

L ANDON CARTER was the son of Col. John Carter and his wife Elizabeth Taylor. He was born in Virginia, January 29, 1760. His father moved to the Watauga Settlement very early and was one of the Thirteen Commissioners in 1772.

Landon Carter was educated at Liberty Hall, North Carolina (now Davidson College), and at an early age began to take an active part in the affairs of the frontier settlement. He served in the Revolutionary War and was at the battle of King's Mountain.

In 1782, he was appointed one of the district auditors for Washington and Sullivan Counties, by the General Assembly of North Carolina, and two years later represented Washington County, in the North Carolina legislature. He was secretary of the first convention for organizing the State of Franklin, and was elected speaker of the Senate of the State of Franklin.

He was Lieutenant-Colonel of the Washington County Militia, and represented that county in the first constitutional convention of the State of Tennessee.

Carter County was named in honor of Col. Landon Carter, and the county seat Elizabethton takes its name from his wife who was Elizabeth Maclin. They were married February 26, 1784, and were the parents of seven children.

Col. Landon Carter died January 6, 1800, and is buried in the Carter cemetery near Elizabethton, Tennessee.

EDMUND WILLIAMS

Edmund Williams, one of the early settlers of the watauga region, was a native of Wales. He emmigarted first to Massachusetts, where he married Lucretia Adams, and later moved with his family to North Carolina, where he was living in Washington County, in 1778.

In 1782, he was a member of the court of Washington County, and during this year was appointed one of the districts auditors of Washington and Sullivan Counties by the general assemblyof the state of North Carolina.

During the struggle between the organizers of the State of Franklin and the mother State of North Carolina, Edmund Williams was one of the magistrates at a court held by the North Carolina faction, at the home of William Davis, in February, 1787. By next (1788) he served as sheriff of Washington County, State of Franklin.

Later, in 1790, at the first term of the Washington County Court, held in the territory Southwest of the Ohio River, Edmund Williams was present as magistrate.

Edmund Williams was a large land owner. and entered several tracts of fine farm land on Buffalo Creek, in Washington County. He was a devout Baptist and was an active member of the Old Sinking Springs Baptist Church. This sturdy pioneer died in the autumn of 1795, and is buried on the site of his old homestead, on the banks of Buffalo Creek, opposite of Buffalo Mountain. He was the father of eight children.

NORTH CAROLINA REVULOTUIONARY ARMY ACCOUNTS

Index to Soldiers

Residing in Washington and Sullivan Counties

1781-1783

An account of Specie certificates paid into the Comptroller's office by John Armstrong, Entry taker, for lands in North Carolina taken from Accounts paid by Anthony Bledsoe, Edmund Williams, and Landon Carter.

Note: -The numerial following the soldiers names here listed refer to volume, page and folio of the North Carolina Revolutionary Army Accounts in the State Archives at Raleigh, N.C.

Adams, Jonathan, I-36-4
Adams, Micajah, I-36-2; I-36-2
Adams, Will, V-103-2
Adkins, Charles, I-10-4
Adkins, Chas., I-72-4
Alandrew, David, I-13-2
Alexander, David, I-21-2; I-63-4
Alexander, J., XII-89-4
Alexander, Jacob, I-47-2
Alexander, Jos., I-1-4
Alexander, Thomas, I-12-4
Allison, Charles, I-3-2
Allison, John, I-5-2; I-28-2; I-72-4;
    I-90-2
Allison, Robert, I-12-4; I-12-4
Allison, Will, I-61-2
Allison, William, I-14-2; I-65-4
Anderson, Barney, I-8-2
Anderson, Chas., XII-74-2
Anderson, Isaac, I-66-2
Anderson, James, I-90-2
Anderson, Jno., I-61-4
Anderson, John, I-74-4
Armstrong, James, I-30-2; I-74-2
Armstrong, Lancelot, I-1-4
Armstrong, Lanty, I-13-2; I-13-4
Arnett, Jacob, I-8-4
Arnold, John, I-10-2
Arnold, Nathan, I-13-2
Aronwine, John, I-61-2; XII-50-2
Arthur, Matthew, I-82-4
Asher, Charles, I-9-4
Asher, John, I-30-2
Asher, Will, I-36-2
Ashherst, Wm., I-30-2
Ashert, Chas., I-9-4
Ashert, John, I-9-4
Ashert, Will, I-9-4
Ashmore, Hezekiah, I-3-2
Austin, John, I-10-4; I-19-4; I-74-2
Bacon, Will, I-17-2

Bailey, David, I-46-4
Bailey, Hezekiah, I-23-4
Bailey, James, I-1-2
Bailey, Robert, I-23-2
Baits, John, I-62-2
Baker, Bolin, I-7-2
Baker, Bollen, I-16-4
Baker, F., XII-89-4
Barker, Austin, I-63-2
Barker, Francis, I-24-4
Barker, George, I-89-2
Barker, Thomas, I-27-4
Barker, William, I-59-4
Barren, Henry, I-20-2
Barren, James, I-19-4
Barren, Will, I-20-2
Barrett, John, I-10-4
Barrett, Reubin, I-10-4
Barrin, Henry, I-19-4
Barrin, James, I-19-4
Barrin, John, I-28-2
Bartin, J., XII-89-4
Baskins, John, I-5-2; I-7-2; I-63-2
Bayly, Robert, I-23-4
Bealer, Daniel, I-61-4
Bealer, Dan'l, I-61-4
Bealer, Jacob, I-14-2; I-14-2
Bealer, John, I-14-2; I-61-4
Bealer, Joseph, I-14-2
Bealer, Ubrick, I-61-4
Bealer, Jacob, XII-20-4
Bean, R., XII-89-4; XII-90-2
Bean, W., XII-90-2
Beane, Edmund, I-60-2
Beard, Hugh, I-10-2; I-13-2
Becar, Edmund, I-20-2
Becar, Robert, I-20-2
Been, Edmund, I-19-4
Been, George, I-23-4
Been, Jesse, I-25-4
Been, John, I-23-4

Been, Robert, I-19-4
Been, Will, I-19-2
Bennett, John, I-9-4
Bennett, Thomas, I-7204; I-72-4; I-72-4
Berry, James, I-74-2; I-74-2
Bershears, Sam'l, I-61-4
Billings, Will, I-5-4
Bird, A., XII-89-4
Bird, Amos, I-8-4; I-8-4; I-9-2; V-97-2
Bird, Geo., XII-73-4
Bird, John, I-8-4
Bird, Johnathan, I-14-2
Bird, Jos., I-17-2; I-63-2
Birdwell, Ben., I-9-4
Birdwell, Benjamin, I-2-2
Bishop, Jonas, XII-16-4
Bishop, Jones, I-51-2
Bishop, Matthew, I-79-4
Bishop, Stephen, I-73-4
Bishurs, Philip, I-11-4
Black, John, I-72-4
Black, Jno., I-48-2; XII-18-4
Black, Rodger, I-66-2
Blackburn, Robert, V-100-4
Blackwell, David, I-59-2
Blair, Alex., I-48-2; I-58-4; I-62-2
Blair, Alexander, I-61-4
Blair, Hugh, I-11-2; I-56-4
Blair, James, I-15-2
Blair, John, I-62-2
Blevins, John, I-15-2
Blythe, John, I-59-4
Boiland, Wm., I-23-4
Boilston, Wm., I-11-4
Boilstone, I-14-2
Boilstone, Jas., I-16-2
Boilstone, James, I-14-2; I-17-2
Boilstone, Sam., I-14-2
Boilstone, Sam'l, I-9-2; I-17-2

Bolding, Elisha, I-10-2
Bond, Ben, I-60-4
Bond, Geo., I-11-4; I-61-4; I-62-2
Bond, George, I-14-2
Border, Michael, I-2-4
Boreas, Thomas, I-5-4
Bounds, Joseph, I-34-2
Bounds, James, I-13-2; I-6302; I-73-4
Bowlin, Will, I-7-2
Box, Edw'd, I-4-2
Box, Henry, I-11-4
Box, John, I-63-4
Box, Jos., I-7-2
Box, Joseph, I-9-2
Boyd, John, I-8-4
Boyd, Will, I-10-2
Boyd, Wm., I-10-2
Boyer, Luke, I-4-4
Boyldson, James, I-4-4
Boylstone, Wm., I-67-2
Bradshaw, John, I-59-4
Bragg, Joseph, I-21-4
Brannon, Thomas, I-51-2
Brantley, Charles, I-1-2; I-1-4 (3)
Brarfield, Josa., I-23-4
Brashers, Philip, I-14-2
Brawfield, Josa., I-9-2
Bread, Avery, I-9-2
Breed, Avery, I-16-2; I-16-4; I-17-2
Brock, Allen, I-13-2 (2)
Brock, James, I-13-2; V-92-4; V-93-2
Broils, Louis, I-14-2; I-46-4
Brooks, Geo., I-6-4 (2); I-58-2
Brooks, Littleton, I-29-4
Brooks, Thomas, I-1-2
Brooks, Will, I-61-2
Brooks, William, I-1-4
Brown, Alsolom, XII-16-4

Brown, B., XII-89-4

Brown, David, I-16-4

Brown, Hugh, I-9-2

Brown, J., XII-14-2

Brown, Jacob, I-5-4; I-24-2; I-91-2

Brown, James, I-59-2

Brown, John, I-9-4; I-56-2

Brown, Joseph, I-88-4; V-92-4

Brown, Randolph, I-61-4

Brown, Thomas, I-5-4; I-16-4

Brown, Will, I-15-2

Brown, William, I-3-2

Brown, Wm., I-13-4; V-93-2

Broylstone, Jas., I-59-4

Brumit, John, I-19-2

Brumley, Wm., I-16-4

Brumly, Will, I-17-2

Brummet, Pearson, I-90-2

Brummit, Jno., I-43-4 (2)

Brummit, John, I-56-4

Brundage, Sol, XII-74-4

Bryan, W., XII-14-2

Buchannon, Jno., I-61-4

Bullard, Isaac, I-7-2 (2)

Bullard, Israel, I-7-2

Bullard, Jesse, I-82-4

Bullard, Joseph, I-7-2 (3); I-20-2

Buller, Isaac, I-7-2

Buller, Jno., I-58-2

Buller, Joseph, I-82-2

Bullock, Richd., I-23-4

Bumps, Jos., I-24-2

Bunch, John, XII-16-4

Burch, Richard, I-10-4

Burke, Jos., I-9-5

Burner, Sam, I-41-4

Burnes, James, I-34-4

Burney, Samuel, I-2-2

Bussle, Jacob, XII-74-2

Butler, Elisha, I-19-4

Butler, Joseph, I-4-2

Butler, Will, V-92-4

Byram, Ebenezar, I-21-2; I-61-2; I-73-2

Byram, Ebenezar, I-73-2

Cain, Aquilla, I-1-4

Cair, Will, I-27-4

Caldwell, Andrew, I-7-4

Caldwell, Thomas, I-52-2 (3)

Caldwell, William, I-8-2

Callahan, Joel, I-16-4

Calliham, Joel, I-46-4

Callihan, Joel, I-47-2

Calvert, Fred'k, I-56-2

Calvit, Fred'k, XII-18-4

Calvit, John, I-56-2

Calvit, Will, I-56-2; XII-18-4

Calwell, John, I-73-2

Cameron, James, I-13-2

Campbell, Alex., I-29-4 (2); I-41-4; I-74-2 (4)

Campbell, Alexander, I-8-2

Campbell, Alex'r, I-13-4; I-21-4

Campbell, Charles, I-29-4

Campbell, David, I-10-2 (2); I-21-4; I-29-4; I-52-2; I-61-2

Campbell, James, I-3-2; I-16-2 (2); I-52-2 (2); I-61-2; I-61-4; I-74-2 (3)

Campbell, Jas., I-16-2; I-61-2

Campbell, John, I-8-2; I-16-2; I-57-2

Campbell, Jno., I-27-4

Campbell, Robert, I-73-2 ; I-74-2 (3)

Campbell, Soloman, I-81-4

Campbell, Will, I-41-2

Carmack, John, I-24-2; I-90-4

Carmack, Jno., I-24-2

Carpenter, Boston, I-73-2

Carpenter, Waldrick, I-2-4

Carr, James, I-28-4

Carr, Will, I-46-4

Carriger, Nichs., I-65-4

Carrill, Ben., V-100-4

Carrington, Timothy, I-63-4

Carryer, Jona., I-16-4

Carson, Will, I-27-4

Carson, Wm., I-27-4

Carter, Caleb, I-11-2 (2); I-11-4; I-14-2

Carter, Daniel, I-11-2

Carter, Emmanuel, I-81-2 (2)

Carter, Jacob, I-11-2

Carter, Jesse, I-13-4

Carter, John, I-11-2 (2); I-11-4; I-24-2

Carter, Landon, I-23-2; I-81-2; I-81-4

Carter, Levi, I-80-2

Carter, Michael, I-21-4

Carter, Michel, I-10-2

Carter, Mich'l, I-11-2; I-61-2; I-80-2

Carter, Nathan'l, I-61-2

Caruthers, And's, XII-74-2

Caruthers, Sam'l, XII-74-2

Cashedy, John, I-24-2

Cassidy, John, I-2-2 (2)

Casson, Cha's, I-7-4

Cassum, John, I-74-4

Cavall, John, V-107-2

Chamberlain, Andrew, I-34-2

Chamberlain, Jeremiah, I-20-4

Chamberlain, John, I-20-4

Chambers, James, I-9-4 (2)

Chambers, John, I-8-2; I-9-2

Chisolm, John, I-56-2

Chisom, Elijah, I-58-2; I-61-4

Choate, David, I-47-2

Chote, Greenberry, I-2-4

Chote, Isaac, I-5-2

Christian, G., XII-16-4

Christian, Gilbert, XII-8-2

Cisco, John, I-7-4

Clamon, Jno, I-51-2

Clark, Barnes, I-47-2

Clark, Barns, I-90-2

Clark, Geo., I-34-2

Clark, John, I-2-4; I-24-4

Clark, Will, I-24-4

Clark, William, I-2-4

Clarke, John, I-23-2; I-81-4

Clarke, Will, I-23-4

Clasbey, James, I-46-4

Clendinning, James, I-61-4

Clendinning, John, I-61-4

Cloud, Jessee, I-6-4

Cloud, Jere, I-6-4

Coal, Joseph, I-89-2

Cobb, Arthur, I-16-4

Coble, Drenin, I-20-2

Cock, John, XII-3-2

Cogle, Robert, I-11-4

Cohorn, John, XII-73-4; XII-74-2

Coil, Robert, I-72-4

Coldwell, Will, I-12-4

Coldwell, William, XII-7-2

Coleman, Will, I-3-4; I-4-2

Collet, Isaac, I-13-2

Colvert, Wm., I-23-4

Colvil, Tho., I-56-2

Colwell, Wm., I-40-2

Condry, Rich'd, I-60-4

Conway, Philip, I-13-2

Cook, Thomas, I-20-2

Cooper, James, I-10-4; I-19-4

Cooper, Philip, I-59-4

Copeland, Zacha, I-66-2 (2); I-66-4

Cortney, Ben, I-56-2

Cortney, John, I-3-2

Cortney, Micajah, I-1-2

Cortney, Will, I-62-2

Cortney, William, I-1-2

Cosson, John, I-9-4

Cotton, Young, I-30-2; V-106-2

Couch, Christopher, XII-16-4
Courtney, John, XII-7-2
Cowen, Andrew, V-96-4 (2)
Cowen, John, I-3-2
Cowen, Robert, I-4-4; I-67-4
Cox, Edward, I-32-2
Cox, John, XII-50-2 (2)
Cox, Joseph, I-21-4; I-79-4
Cox, Richard, XII-73-4
Cox, Samuel, I-60-4
Cox, Thomas, I-50-4; XII-74-2
Cox, Will, XII-18-4
Cox, William, I-1-4; I-65-4 (2)
Cox, Wm., I-39-4
Coyle, Robert, I-40-2; I-42-2 (2); I-60-4
Crabb, John, I-77-2; XII-74-2
Crabb, Jos., XII-73-4
Craddock, David, I-66-2
Craft, J., XII-90-2
Crage, John, I-74-4
Craig, David, I-36-4
Craig, James, XII-20-4
Craige, J., XII-73-4
Craike, Thomas, I-3-2
Crawford, Isaac, I-16-4; I-17-2; I-59-4
Crawford, Moses, I-16-2
Crawford, Sam., I-47-2
Crawford, Thomas, I-16-2
Crawford, Thos., I-9-2; I-16-4
Crawford, Will, I-16-2
Cremor, Dan'l, I-2-4
Crocket, Robert, I-7-4; I-24-2; I-51-2
Crockett, John, I-57-2
Crockett, Jno., I-7-2
Crockett, Rob., I-47-2
Crofford, Isaac, I-14-2
Crofford, Samuel, I-81-4
Cross, Abram, V-93-2

Culberson, Jos., I-3-2
Culberson, Joseph, I-82-4
Cummins, Jos., I-7-2
Cunningham, John, I-5-4
Cunningham, Will, I-8-4
Currey, Sam, I-15-2
Dail, Will, I-47-2
Dailey, Thomas, I-34-2
Daily, Will, I-38-2
Dalton, John, I-17-4
Danham, Jos., I-17-4
Daniel, Francis, I-15-2
Daniel, Will, I-50-2
Darbery, Hugh, I-2-2
Davidson, Jos., I-19-4
Davidson, Joseph, I-7-4
Davies, Samuel, V-97-2
Davies, Will, I-5-2
Davies, Isaac, I-18-2; I-23-4; XII-16-4
Davis, Jas., I-59-2
Davis, Joseph, I-67-2
Davis, Nathan'l, V-93-2
Davis, Nath'l, I-5-2; I-24-2
Davis, Robert, I-18-2
Davis, Sam, I-63-4
Davis, Thomas, I-3-2
Davis, Will, I-5-2; I-9-4; I-24-4 (2); I-47-2; I-74-4
Day, Will, I-62-4; I-63-2
Dayley, Geo., I-59-2
Deadman, Jeremiah, I-28-2; I-64-4
Decon, Wm., I-66-2
Delany, Dan., I-14-2
Delany, Danl., V-100-2
Delany, Jas., I-59-4
Delany, John, I-1-4; I-13-2
Delany, Jos., XII-50-2
Delany, Will., XII-20-4
Dennam, David, I-28-2
Denney, Alex'r, I-44-2

Denten, Jona., I-43-4

Denton, Abraham, I-90-2

Denton, John, I-7-4; I-20-2

Denton, Sam'l, I-63-4

Denton, Samuel, I-7-2 (2); I-7-4; I-20-2; I-23-4

Denton, Thomas, I-20-2

Depreast, W., I-47-2

Detson, William, I-10-4

Dickson, James, I-50-2

Ditson, John, V-97-2

Dixon, Jas., I-40-2

Dixon, John, I-80-2

Dixon, Thomas, I-12-4

Dobson, Jos., I-19-4

Dobson, Rawligh, I-56-2

Doddy, Howell, I-1-2; I-3-4; I-4-2; I-11-2; I-16-2

Dodson, Lazarus, I-89-2

Dogett, Geo., V-107-2

Dogget, Geo., I-10-4

Doghead, John, I-1-4

Doghed, John, I-10-2; I-10-4

Doghed, Miller, I-10-2

Doherty, Geo., I-2-4 (2); I-88-4

Doherty, William, I-2-4; I-13-2 (2)

Donohoo, John, I-74-2

Dotey, Azariah, I-4-2; I-74-4

Dotey, Jos., I-19-4

Dotson, John, V-97-2

Dotson, Wm., I-51-2

Dougan, Hugh, I-67-2

Douglas, James, I-62-2

Douglas, Sam, XII-18-4

Drake, Michael, I-62-4

Dugan, Dan'l, I-67-2

Duggar, Julius, I-74-4

Duglas, Jno., I-24-2

Duglas, Jonothan, V-99-2

Duncan, John, I-51-4; V-93-2

Duncan, Joseph, V-93-2

Duncan, Patrick, I-9-4

Dunder, John, I-62-2

Dunderhow, John, I-74-2

Dunham, David, I-16-4

Dunham, Hardin, I-28-2; I-52-2

Dunham, Jos., I-59-2; I-60-2

Dunham, Joseph, I-21-4; I-59-4

Dunham, Reubin, I-17-4

Dunken, John, I-36-4

Dunn, Joseph, I-2-4; I-4-2; I-5-4

Durham, Cravens, I-44-2

Durham, James, I-74-4

Durham, Jos., I-16-4

Dyer, Francis, I-15-2; I-25-2

Eadons, James, I-56-4

Eagleston, David, I-12-4

Early, Thomas, I-3-2; I-82-2 (2)

Easley, Jos., XII-20-4

Eastis, George, I-89-2

Edmonds, Rich'd, I-16-2; XII-74-2

Edwards, Edmund, I-19-4

Edwards, Evan, I-79-4

Edwards, Jacob, I-1-2 (2); I-18-2; I-58-4

Edwards, James, I-63-4

Edwards, John, I-43-2

Edwards, Jonathan, I-1-2

Edwards, Thomas, I-10-4

Eller, Jos., I-13-4

Ellett, Thomas, I-38-4

Elliot, Hugh, V-106-2

Elliott, James, I-50-4; I-52-2; I-65-4

Elliott, James, I-23-4

Elliott, Simon, V-106-2 (2)

Elliott, William, V-106-2 (2)

Ellis, John, I-19-4; XII-24-2

Ellison, James, I-63-2

Ellison, Robert, I-17-2

Ellit, Geo., I-50-4

England, Will, I-16-4

English, And's, I-43-4 (2)

English, James, I-3-2; I-10-4
English, Jas., I-47-2
English, Joshua, I-4-2 (3)
English, Wm., I-6-4
Epperson, Thomas, I-10-4; I-28-2
Erly, James, I-36-2
Evans, John, I-3-2 (2); I-16-4
Evans, Jos., I-6-4
Evans, Nathan'l, I-30-2; I-72-4
Evans, Nath'l, I-6-4; I-11-2
Fagon, John, I-34-4
Fain, Eben, I-24-2
Fain, Ebenezer, I-6-4
Fain, Nicholas, I-62-4
Fain, Samuel, I-82-2; V-100-4
Fain, William, I-81-4 (2)
Farguson, Aaron, I-59-4
Faris, William, I-1-4
Farrill, Smith, I-2-4
Faulkner, Wm., I-8-4
Fears, Jona, I-2-4
Ferguson, Aaron, I-16-4
Ferguson, Moses, I-16-4; I-59-4
Ferguson, Wm., I-4-4
Fergusson, Aaron, I-27-4
Ferrill, Smith, I-34-4
Finn, Peter, I-12-4
Fitts, Jno., I-37-4
Fitzgerald, Jarratt, I-1-4
Flannery, William, I-65-4
Flannery, Wm., I-8-4
Flemming, Ralf, I-73-2
Flemming, Ralph, XII-16-4
Fletcher, A., XII-89-4
Fletcher, Gold, I-81-4
Fletcher, Richard, XII-18-4
Flippan, Thomas, I-7-4; I-20-2
Ford, Ben, I-13-4
Ford, Joseph, I-9-4
Forkner, Will, I-60-4
Fowler, Will, I-61-4 (2)

Fowler, William, I-1-2
Francisco, Jacob, I-16-2
Franklin, David, I-72-4
Franklin, John, I-72-4
French, Mason, I-34-4
Fryatt, Thomas, I-8-2
Fryer, Daniel, I-61-2
Fulkerson, John, I-74-4
Fuller, Hugh, I-5-2
Galleker, Tho., I-2-4
Gann, Adam, I-15-4
Gann, Clem, I-15-4 (2)
Gann, Nathan, I-7-2; I-80-2; I-90-2
Gann, Thomas, I-15-4
Garland, Jesse, I-9-2
Garland, John, XII-84-2
Garmon, Hyram, I-73-2
Garner, Jacob, I-36-2
Garner, Walter, I-17-4
Gaskins, Matthew, I-63-4
Gates, William, I-14-2
Gaucher, Jno., I-16-2
Gentry, C., XII-89-4
Gentry, Jesse, I-8-2 (5)
Gentry, Robert, I-8-2; I-59-2
Gest, B., I-47-2
Gest, Ben, I-17-4
Gest, Benja., I-10-2
Gest, Jno., I-47-2
Gest, John, I-16-2; I-17-2
Gest, Jos., I-17-4
Gest, Joseph, I-21-2; V-97-2
Gest, Thomas, I-16-2
Geste, John, I-12-4
Geste, Jos., I-16-4
Geste, Thomas, I-17-2
Gibson, Ben., I-7-4; I-20-2; I-48-4
Gibson, Humphry, I-7-2; I-16-2
Gibson, James, I-4-4; I-5-2 (2); I-5-4; I-36-2
Gilbraith, Alex, I-38-2

Gill, John, V-108-2
Gill, Jno., I-23-4
Gillahan, John, V-98-4
Giller, James, I-15-2
Gillespie, Geo., I-18-2
Gillespie, Thomas, I-2-4; I-5-2; I-8-4; I-10-2; I-10-4; I-11-2; I-20-2
Gillespie, Thos., I-41-2
Gisst, Thomas, I-41-4
Gist, John, I-17-4; I-19-4
Gist, Jno., I-47-2
Gist, Joseph, I-19-4
Gist, Thomas, I-19-4
Glaze, Thomas, V-92-4
Goatcher, John, I-21-2
Gocher, Henry, XII-20-4
Gocher, John, I-17-4
Golchon, John, I-4-4
Golliher, Tho., I-67-2
Good, Will, I-19-4
Goode, William, I-1-2
Goodwin, Alex'r, I-11-4
Goodwin, Ben, I-11-4
Goodwin, James, I-11-2 (2); I-11-4
Goodwin, Richard, I-23-4
Goodwin, Thomas, I-11-4; I-73-2
Goodwin, Thos., I-11-2
Gouch, Nathan, I-73-4
Graham, David, XII-74-2
Graham, James, I-3-2
Graig, Nathan, XII-20-4
Gray, James, I-67-2
Gray, Moulton, I-14-2
Gray, Robert, I-51-2; I-67-2
Gray, Will, I-20-2
Gray, Wm., I-23-2; I-27-2
Grear, John, I-4-4
Greaves, John, I-9-4
Greaves, Patrick, XII-16-2
Green, Francis, I-81-4

Green, Jesse, I-12-4; I-38-2; I-41-4; I-49-4
Green, J., XII-89-2
Green, Josa, I-46-4
Greer, Alexander, I-81-4
Greer, Andrew, I-74-4; I-81-4
Greer, Jesse, I-11-2
Greer, John, I-27-2; I-67-2
Greer, Jos., I-60-2
Greer, Joseph, XII-28-2
Greer, Thomas, I-11-2
Greer, Walter, I-59-4
Greer, William, I-9-4
Greer, Wm., I-5-2
Gregory, James, I-24-2; I-24-4
Grimes, Dav., I-6-4
Grimes, Ephraim, I-77-2 (2)
Grisam, Will, I-72-4
Haggarty, Henry, I-29-4
Hagin, John, I-66-2
Hail, Nicholas, I-82-2
Hail, Nich's., I-19-4
Hail, Shadrack, I-51-2; I-58-4; I-89-2
Hail, Thomas, I-10-4
Hail, Will, I-50-2
Haines, Andrew, I-5-4; I-10-2
Hainey, David, XII-16-4; XII-20-4
Hainley, Francis, I-36-2
Hair, Jos., I-61-4
Haislet, Wm., I-23-2
Hall, Mary, I-82-4
Hallums, Will, I-82-2
Ham, Thomas, I-2-4
Hamilton, F., XII-88-2
Hamilton, Fran's, I-7-2; I-11-2; V-59-2
Hamilton, Jacob, I-10-2
Hamilton, John, I-8-4
Hamilton, Jos., I-30-2
Hamilton, Thomas, I-1-4

Hamilton, William, I-1-4; XII-3-2
Haney, Francis, I-24-2
Haney, Francis, I-36-4
Hannah, Andrew, I-17-2
Hannah, Robert, I-17-2
Hanshaw, John, I-73-2
Harden, John, I-73-2
Hardiman, Tho., I-47-4
Hardiman, Thos., I-47-2; I-51-4
Hardin, Ben, I-21-2; I-54-4; V-92-4; V-101-2
Hardin, John, I-58-2
Hardin, Joseph, I-14-2; I-59-4; I-79-4
Hardin, Jos., I-24-2
Harris, Edward, XII-7-2 (2)
Harris, Stephen, I-17-2
Harrison, Gideon, I-23-4
Harriss, Stephen, I-62-4
Hathhorn, Noah, I-41-2
Hatton, Will, V-98-4 (2)
Hatton, Wm., V-98-4
Hawkins, Aaron, I-5-2
Hawkins, Nicholas, I-24-2
Haygin, Barney, L-2-2
Haynes, Richard, I-46-4
Hays, Andrew, I-4-2
Hays, John, I-13-2
Hayslet, Wm., I-24-2
Head, Wm., XII-74-2
Headpseth, Ralph., I-90-2
Heany, David, XII-20-4
Hear, Joseph, I-61-4
Heard, John, I-3-4
Hedden, Elisha, I-67-2
Heddin, Elisha, I-11-2; I-73-2
Heddin, Levi, I-73-2
Hellams, William, I-88-4
Hellims, David, I-58-4
Henderson, Dan, I-52-2; I-41-2 (3)
Henderson, Jas., I-4-2

Henderson, John, I-53-2; I-58-2; I-82-4
Henderson, Joseph, I-11-2; I-17-4
Henderson, Thomas, I-4-2; I-15-2; I-74-2
Hendricks, Solo., I-3-4
Hendricks, Soloman, I-3-4
Henly, Henry, XII-18-4
Henny, James, XII-20-4
Henry, Hugh, I-55-4
Henry, James, I-36-2
Henry, Samuel, V-92-4; I-12-4
Henry Saml., I-12-4; I-63-4
Herndon, Joseph, I-61-2
Hershie, John, I-73-2
Hetherly, Nevius, XII-1-2
Hichcock, Jno., I-9-4
Hichcock, John, I-63-4
Hicks, Henry, V-92-4
Hicks, Mesheek, I-36-2
Hicks, Saml., V-108-2
Hicks, Samuel, I-7-4
Hicks, Will, I-36-2
Hider, Mich'l, I-9-4
Higgins, Edward, I-2-4
Hightower, Austin, I-4-2
Hightower, John, I-4-4
Hightower, Oldham, I-9-4
Hightower, Ozbon, I-73-2
Hightower, Richard, I-1-4
Hill, Abram, I-14-2; I-16-4
Hill, Dan'l, I-17-4
Hill, Isaac, I-10-2
Hill, John, I-47-2 (2)
Hill, Thomas, '-61-4
Hix, Abenego, I-5-2
Hix, Elijah, I-79-4
Hix, Meshich, I-5-2
Hix, Will, I-5-2
Hix, William, I-17-4
Hobdaway, Timothy, I-10-2

Hodge, Ambrose, I-2-2 (2)
Hodge, Francis, I-24-2
Hohamer, Henry, I-34-4
Holebrook, Wm., I-5-2
Hohimer, Henry, I-19-2
Holliway, William, I-K4-2
Holloway, John, I-72-4
Holloway, Will, I-20-2
Holly, Francis, I-2-4
Holly, John, I-36-2; V-97-2; V-98-4
Holly, Jona., I-2-4
Hopton, John, I-13-2
Hook, Elisha, XII-7-2
Hoskins, Elias, I-11-2; I-62-4; I-74-4
Hoskins, Jesse, I-9-4; I-10-2
Hoskins, Jessey, I-81-4
Hoskins, Jno., I-74-2
Hoskins, John, I-74-4
Hoskins, Nehemiah, I-48-4
Houghton, Will, I-50-2
Houston, James, I-21-4
Houston, John, I-80-2
Howard, Abram, I-7-4; I-46-2; XII-74-4
Howard, John, I-7-4 (3)
Howard, Thomas, V-97-2
Howe, John, I-11-4
Hubbard, James, I-3-2
Hubbart, James, I-34-2
Hudson, Geo., I-23-2; I-57-2
Hudson, Nancy, XII-18-4
Hughes, David, I-12-4
Hughes, J., XII-89-4
Hughes, James, V-108-2
Hughes, John, I-5-4; I-57-2; I-82-2
Hughes, Stephen, I-16-2
Hughston, Jas., I-41-4
Hukey, David, XII-16-4
Humphries, Talph, I-81-4
Humphries, Richard, I-4-2

Hunt, Esly, I-13-4
Hunt, Moses, I-20-4; I-82-2
Hunt, Tho., I-16-4
Hunter, Demsey, I-81-2; I-81-4
Hunter, Edward, I-36-2 (2); I-36-4; I-50-4
Hunter, Moses, I-73-2
Hunter, Tho., I-51-4
Hunter, Thomas, I-48-4
Husband, Hiram, XII-7-2
Huse, Henry, I-62-2
Huston, John, I-21-4
Hutchins, Smith, I-7-2 (2); I-27-4; I-72-4
Hutton, Wm., V-98-4
Hygins, Edward, I-82-2
Ingland, Chas., I-72-4
Ingland, John, I-73-4; I-74-2
Inglish, Joshua, V-107-2
Inglish, Will, I-61-2
Ingram, Will, I-24-2
Inman, Abednego, I-59-4
Ireland, John, I-2-2
Irwin, David, I-62-2
Isbell, Zacha, I-48-2
Jack, Jeremiah, I-82-2
Jackson, John, XII-74-2
Jett, Stephen, I-56-2
Joab, Will, I-3-4
Job, Sam'l, I-19-4
Jobe, Samuel, I-1-2
Johnson, David, I-4-2
Johnson, James, V-98-4
Johnson, Kinsey, I-59-4
Johnson, Moses, I-10-2
Jonakin, Thomas, I-19-4
Jones, Henry, I-4-2; I-4-4
Jones, Charles, I-89-2
Jones, James, I-77-2
Jones, John, I-4-2 (2); I-4-4
Jones, Joseph, I-73-4 (2); XII-16-4

Jones, Phil., XII-14-2
Jones, Philip, I-2-2
Jones, Rob., XII-89-4
Jones, Thomas, I-15-2; XII-20-4
Jonikin, Thomas, I-34-4
Jonkin, Thomas, I-19-4
Jordan, Thomas, I-23-4
Karling, Edward, I-74-2
Keener, Rodcham, I-1-4
Keeney, John, I-60-2
Keenor, Rodham, I-82-2
Keeny, John, I-16-2; I-17-4; I-59-4
Keeny, Jos., I-16-4
Keith, Alexander, I-72-4
Keith, Daniel, I-72-4
Kelcey, Alex., I-61-2
Kelcey, Hugh, I-34-2 (2)
Kellam, Seth, I-62-2
Keller, Daniel, V-99-2
Kellum, Job, I-1-2
Kellum, John, I-1-2
Kelly, Alex'r, I-12-4 (2)
Kelser, Sam, I-7-4
Kenady, Moses, I-89-2
Kennedy, John, I-28-4
Kennedy, Moses, I-8-4; I-14-2; I-24-2
Kennerly, John, V-108-2
Kenor, Francis, I-82-4
Kerchaval, Jno., I-48-4 (2)
Kerdendall, John, I-5-2
Kerr, Geo., I-13-2; I-23-4
Kerr, James, I-72-4
Kesiah, Standefer, I-47-2
Keywood, John, XII-50-2
Kinder, Jno., I-47-2
King, Henry, I-60-4
King, James, I-62-2; I-72-4
King, Jas., I-13-4
King, Jonathan, I-60-4

King, Robert, I-1-2 (2); I-1-4; I-61-4; I-62-2
King, T., XII-90-2
King, Thomas, I-61-4
King, Will, XII-50-2
Kinsey, Tho., I-7-4; I-48-4
Kinsey, Thos., I-16-4
Kisiah, Sanders, I-7-4
Kirk, Joseph, I-2-4
Kirkendall, Adam, I-23-2
Kirkendall, Benj., I-82-2
Kirkendall, James, I-5-2; I-12-4
Kirkendall, Jno., I-4-4
Kirkendall, Jona., I-10-2
Kirkendall, Jonathan, I-34-2
Kirkendall, Jos., I-4-4
Kirkendall, Sampson, V-107-2
Kirkland, John, I-60-4
Knave, J., XII-87-4
Lackey, Adam, I-9-4
Lackey, James, I-10-2
Lane, Corbin, I-17-2
Lane, Dutton, I-13-4; I-6-4
Lane, Equilla, I-1-4
Lane, Isaac, I-19-4
Lane, John, I-10-4
Lane, Tidance, I-34-4
Lane, Tidings, I-19-4
Langineir, Chas., I-81-4
Langley, James, I-19-4
Langley, Moses, I-10-2
Laughlin, James, I-15-2
Lauglin, James, I-13-4 (2); I-15-2
Lauglin, Thomas, I-13-4 (2)
Lavrick, Mich'l, I-62-2
Lawson, J., XII-90-2
Lawson, James, I-1-4
Leeper, John, I-13-2 (2)
Leeper, Math'w, I-12-4
Leeper, Matt., I-7-4
Light, Jacob, I-2-2

Light, John, I-19-4
Light, Robert, I-82-2
Lile, David, I-8-2 (2)
Lile, Samuel, I-8-2
Lite, John, I-1-4
Livingston, Sam, XII-74-2
Lockhart, Chas., I-74-4; XII-74-2 (2)
Locus, Austin, I-2-2
Loney, David, XII-73-4
Long, John, I-34-4; I-74-4 (2)
Long, Joseph, I-74-2
Longmier, Charles, I-2-2 (2)
Looney, David, XII-74-2
Looney, Moses, I-30-2
Looney, Robert, I-36-4 (2)
Love, John, I-27-4
Lovelady, J., XII-89-4
Lovelady, Jos., I-13-4; I-17-2
Lovelady, Joseph, I-3-4
Lovelady, Marshall, I-40-2; V-98-4
Lowry, John, I-8-4
Lusk, Robert, V-92-4
Lyle, David, I-59-2
Lyle, Sam'l, XII-16-4
Mace, William, I-65-4 (2)
Madcap, William, I-82-2
Magahee, Farrell, I-16-4
Magahee, Nath'l, I-82-2
Magehee, Terrell, V-97-2
Maghan, James, I-11-4
Maglochlan, Alex., I-25-4
Mahon, D., XII-73-4
Mahoney, Michael, I-2-2
Menascoe, James, I-34-2
Maney, Martin, I-14-2
Marshall, Bartly, I-46-4
Marshall, Wm., I-74-2
Martin, And'w, I-21-2
Martin, G., XII-90-2
Martin, Geo., I-21-2
Martin, George, I-8-4

Martin, James, I-65-4; I-90-2
Martin, John, I-14-2
Martin, Jos., XII-74-2
Martin, Philip, I-56-2
Martin, Richard, V-98-4 (3)
Mason, W., XII-89-4
Mathews, Obediah, I-17-4
Matlock, James, I-77-2; I-90-4
Matthews, Joel, I-9-2
Matthews, Jon., I-63-4
Matthews, Will, I-4-4
Maxwell, Geo., I-36-2; I-36-4
Maxwell, Thomas, I-3-4; I-20-2
Mayers, Adam, V-92-4
Mayfield, Isaac, I-15-4
Mayfield, James, V-93-2
Mayfield, Jno., I-16-2
Mayfield, Randolph, I-17-4; I-21-4;
  I-34-2; I-65-4; V-92-4
Mayson, Will, I-20-2
Meeke, Wm., I-18-2
Meeks, Wm., I-4-4; V-92-4
Mehoney, Mich'l, I-63-2
Middleton, William, I-74-2
Miller, John, I-14-2
Millican, Alex., V-92-4
Millican, James, I-67-2; XII-16-4
  (2); XII-89-4
Mitchell, J., XII-90-2
Mitchell, James, I-1-2; I-8-2
Mitchell, Mark, I-47-2
Mitchell, Thomas, I-3-2; I-44-2
Mitchell, Thos., I-24-2
Mix, William, I-18-2
Mohan, John, I-1-4
Monett, Ben, I-21-4
Mooney, James, I-5-4
Mooney, Thomas, I-90-4
Moore, Abednego, I-39-2
Moore, Alexander, V-107-4
Moore, Charles, I-6-4

Moore, James, I-1-4
Moore, Moses, I-4-4; L-5-2; I-5-4; I-59-4
Moore, Sam, XII-7-2
Moore, Sam'l, I-59-4 (2)
Moore, Will, I-9-2
Moore, Wm., I-4-4
Moreland, Will, V-103-2
Morgan, Abel, I-21-4
Morgan, Adonijah, I-67-4
Morgan, John, I-72-4
Morgan, Murrey, I-51-2
Morgan, Thomas, I-2-4; I-34-4; V-98-4
Morrell, John, I-15-2
Morrell, Thomas, I-15-2
Morris, Daniel, XII-7-2
Morris, Drury, I-73-4
Morris, Gideon, I-36-2
Morris, Patrick, I-21-4
Morris, Shadrach, I-41-2
Morris, Shadrack, I-3-2; I-36-2
Morrison, Jas., XII-18-4
Morrison, Jno., I-6-4; XII-18-4
Morrison, John, I-6-4; I-62-2; XII-18-4
Morrison, Michael, I-62-2 (2)
Morriss, Drury, I-13-2; V-92-4
Morriss, Drewery, I-38-2
Morriss, Gideon, I-17-2; I-59-2
Morriss, Giddin, I-11-2
Morriss, Shadrach, I-11-2; I-17-2
Morriss, Shadrack, V-92-4
Morrous, Gideon, I-17-4
Moseley, David, I-51-2
Moseley, Ben, I-54-4
Moyors, Chris'n, I-74-4
Muligan, John, I-66-2
Mullin, Flower, I-60-4
Murphy, John, I-10-2; I-10-4
Murphy, Patrick, I-82-4

Murphy, Will, I-3-2; I-10-4; I-14-2; I-47-2
Murrow, Alex, I-16-2
Myet, James, I-7-2
McAdams, James, I-24-2
McAdoo, David, I-23-4 (2)
McAdoo, John, I-67-4
McAdoo, Will, I-36-2
McAdoo, Wm., I-8-4
McBroom, Thos., XII-74-2 (2)
McBroom, Will, I-58-4
McBroom, Wm., XII-74-2 (2)
McCall, Francis, I-62-4; I-67-4
McCartney, Chas., I-7-2; I-7-4
McCartney, Charles, I-7-2 (2); I-20-2
McCartney, James, I-7-2 (2); I-7-4; I-20-2 (2)
McCartney, John, I-20-2 (2)
McCartney, William, I-2-2
McClain, Ephraim, I-81-4
McClain, Robert, I-20-2
McClary, Pat, I-4-4
McClary, Patrick, I-17-2; I-59-4
McClay, J., XII-73-4
McClure, Andrew, I-4-4
McCollum, Isaac, I-20-2
McCollum, Thomas, I-13-2
McCord, David, V-92-4
McCorkle, John, I-24-2
McCorkle, Sam'l, V-99-2
McCormack, Wm., V-99-2
McCrary, Jas., I-56-2
McFarland, Thos., XII-18-4
McFarland, Alexander, I-73-2
McFarlin, Thom., I-17-2
McFarling, Alexander, I-72-4
McFerren, Andrew, I-79-4 (2)
McGaha, Sam'l, I-37-4
McGaha, Samuel, I-15-2
McGaha, Tarrell, I-23-4

McGahee, Samuel, I-5-4
McGehee, Ferrell, I-5-2
McGuire, Nely, I-13-4
McLain, James, XII-18-4
McLaughlin, Hugh, XII-20-4
McLean, Ephraim, I-24-4
McMurray, James, I-41-2
McMurtry, James, I-9-2
McMurty, Jas., I-2-4
McNabb, Babtis, I-2-2
McNabb, David, I-12-4; I-63-4
McNabb, James, I-82-2; I-82-4
McNabb, Jno., I-50-2; I-63-2
McNabb, John, I-2-2 (3); I-2-4
McNabb, Thomas, I-82-4
McNair, James, I-11-4; I-61-4
McName, Peter, I-48-4
McPike, Will, I-46-2
McSpaddin, John, I-3-2
McZephon, Jonas, I-3-2
Naile, Nicholas, I-4-2
Nale, Matthew, I-10-4
Nash, John, I-14-2; I-72-2
Nave, Gabriel, I-17-4; I-18-2;
　V-93-2
Nave, Henry, I-18-2
Nave, John, I-17-4 (2)
Neal, Nich's, I-4-4
Neal, Nicholas, I-82-4
Nelson, Edmond, I-81-4
Nelson, Elisha, V-92-4
Nelson, Southy, I-60-2
Nelson, Southerly, V-92-4
Nelson, William, I-7-4; I-65-4
Newkam, William, I-74-4
Newman, Cornelius, I-17-4
Newman, Jno., I-34-4
Newman, John, I-10-4; I-17-2;
　I-17-4; I-41-2; I-48-4; I-73-2;
　I-82-2; XII-16-4

Nisely, Mich'l, I-39-4
Norris, Sam, I-61-2
Nowe, Gabriel, I-8-2
Nowland, George, I-66-2
Nowland, John, I-72-4; I-82-4
Nowland, Will, I-38-2
Nowlin, John, V-107-2
Nows, Richard, V-97-2
Odle, Job, I-4-2
Odle, Thompson, I-2-2
Odle, Wm., I-3-4
Odul, John, I-4-4
Olliver, Ben, I-56-4
Omsby, James, I-23-4
Oneal, C., XII-90-2
O'Neal, Cornelius, I-17-4
Orr, Robert, I-10-2
Ouslin, John, I-73-2
Owens, Elijah, I-13-4
Owens, Wm., I-4-2
Owins, Will, I-4-4
Parker, Chas., I-67-2
Parker, Will, I-41-2; I-81-4
Parker, William, I-7-4
Parks, Sam, I-47-4
Parmley, Jno., XII-74-2
Parrimore, Ezekiel, I-7-4
Parrimore, Math'w, I-7-2
Parrymore, Amos, I-34-4
Parrymore, Ezekiel, I-46-4
Parrymore, Harmon, I-23-4
Parrymore, Thos., I-47-2
Pate, Matt, I-67-2
Pate, Matthew, I-4-4
Paterson, Jas., I-62-2
Patterson, John, I-5-4; I-59-2;
　I-69-4
Patterson, Jno., I-16-2
Patterson, Robert, I-15-2
Patterson, Will, I-15-2 (2)
Pearce, James, I-59-2; I-59-4

Pearce, Jas., I-59-4

Pearson, Abel, I-17-4; I-73-2; V-93-2

Pearson, Jos., I-7-4

Pebley, Lewis, I-51-4

Pemberton, Jno., XII-20-4

Person, Joseph, I-17-2

Person, Wm., I-5-2

Peters, Chrisley, I-39-4

Peters, Coward, I-39-4

Peters, John, I-39-4 (2)

Peters, Jno., I-39-4

Petrey, Adam, I-61-4

Petrey, John, I-61-4

Phillips, James, I-9-4

Piborn, John, I-17-4

Pibrin, John, I-5-4

Pike, John, I-16-4

Pinson, Joseph, I-67-4

Pinson, Moses, V-92-4

Plemon, Peter, I-1-4

Plumble, Matt, I-82-2

Pointer, Geo., I-51-4

Pope, Jehu, I-8-4; I-34-2

Poston, Elijah, I-14-2

Powers, John, I-7-2 (2)

Prather, Tho., I-15-4

Prather, Will, I-41-2

Prator, Thomas, I-15-4

Prewet, Fuller, I-20-4

Prewet, Isaac, I-20-4

Prewet, Wm., I-20-4

Prewet, Zachariah, I-24-4

Prewett, David, I-7-4

Prewett, Martin, I-5-2; I-5-4

Prewett, Will, I-5-2; I-17-2

Prewett, Zachariah, I-10-2

Prewit, Abraham, I-74-4

Prier, Precedon, I-24-2

Prothero, Alex., I-3-2

Prothero, Alex'r, I-2-4 (3)

Prothero, Alexander, I-7-4

Province, John, I-50-4

Pryor, Pedion, I-15-2

Pursley, Wm., I-27-4

Pussley, Will, I-56-4

Pyborn, John, I-18-2

Pyburn, Ben, I-63-2

Pyburn, John, V-92-4

Richardson, Geo., I-19-4

Richardson, Joseph, I-62-2

Richey, John, I-1-2; I-7-4; I-13-4; I-59-2; V-92-4 (2)

Richey, Jno., I-48-4

Richey, Thomas, V-111-2

Richey, Will, I-16-4

Ridley, Burrly, I-34-4

Ridley, Geo., I-34-4 (4)

Riggs, Edward, I-82-2

Riggs, Reubin, I-56-4; I-62-2

Riggs, Sam'l, I-20-4

Right, John, I-65-4

Risoner, Mich'l, I-47-2

Roan, Hosea, I-16-4 (2)

Roase, Hosea, I-23-4

Robard, Reubin, I-9-2

Roberson, James, I-14-2

Robertson, Charles, I-23-2; XII-16-2; XII-16-4

Robertson, David, I-23-4

Robertson, Isaac, XII-74-2

Robertson, James, I-21-4; XII-16-4; V-107-4

Robinson, E., XII-89-4

Robinson, James, I-65-4

Robinson, Jas., I-46-4

Robinson, John, I-41-4

Robinson, Risdon, I-20-4

Robinson, Will, I-41-2; I-80-2 (2)

Robinson, Wm., I-8-4

Robinson, James, I-7-4; I-51-4

Roddy, James, I-2-2; I-10-2

Rodey, James, I-9-4

Rodolph, Jacob, XII-7-2

Rose, Hose, I-5-2

Roseberry, Will, I-58-2

Rowe, Sol, I-58-4

Ruddle, Randolph, I-3-2

Runnolds, David, I-8-2 (2); I-40-2

Runnolds, Moses, XII-3-2

Runnolds, Will, I-5-2

Russell, George, I-1-4; I-6-4; I-17-4

Russell, Henry, I-17-4

Russell, William, I-89-2

Russell, Wm., I-23-4

Russil, Geo., I-56-4

Rutherford, Ben, I-16-4; I-24-4; I-43-2

Rutherford, Clayborn, I-19-4

Rutledge, Geo., V-96-4 (4)

Ryan, John, XII-74-4

Ryan, Will, I-17-4

Ryan, Wm., I-23-4

Samms, Edward, I-59-4

Samples, Sam, I-8-4; I-17-2

Samples, Samuel, V-107-2

Sampson, Charles, I-82-2

Sams, Edward, I-39-2

Sawyers, John, I-11-4 (2); I-36-2

Scott, Adam, I-9-2 (2)

Scott, John, I-8-4; I-41-4 (2)

Scott, Thomas, I-7-4

Screwer, Jos., XII-16-4

Sedusky, Emanuel, I-15-4; I-74-2

Sellers, Sebert, I-16-2

Seviere, John, I-48-4

Sevier, A., XII-89-4

Sevier, Abram., I-8-4

Sevier, J., XII-89-4

Sevier James, I-23-4; V-107-2

Sevier, Joseph, I-2-4; I-23-2; I-24-4

Sevier, Jos., I-23-2; I-59-2

Sevier, Robert, I-36-2

Sevier, Valentine, I-82-4 (3)

Sevier, Voluntine, I-81-4 (2); I-82-2 (2)

Sharp, A., XII-89-4

Sharp, Thos., I-65-4

Shanks, Holden, I-73-2

Shanks, Holvin, I-73-2

Shanks, Moses, I-73-2 (3)

Shaver, John, I-4-4

Shelby, David, I-64-4; I-81-4

Shelby, Evan, I-24-2; I-61-4

Shelby, John, I-55-4

Sherman, John, I-82-2 (2); I-82-4

Sherrall, Adam, I-8-2; I-59-4; I-63-4

Sherrall, Geo., I-10-4

Sherrall, Philip, V-107-2

Sherrald, Sam'l, I-21-2

Sherrell, Adam, I-4-2; I-9-2

Sherrell, Geo., I-17-2; I-72-4

Sherrell, Jno., I-2-4

Sherrell, John, I-17-2; I-62-4

Sherrell, Sam, I-59-2

Sherrill, Uriah, I-72-4

Shilton, Charles, I-18-2

Shooler, Geo., I-10-4

Shores, Jno., I-16-4

Shortridge, John, V-92-4

Shote, Edward, V-92-4

Sides, Peter, I-14-2

Simmons, Charles, I-24-2

Simmons, Jno., I-16-4

Simpson, Will, I-48-4

Sims, Job, I-73-2 (3); I-73-4

Singletary, Ben, XII-73-4

Sisco, Jacob, I-20-2

Skelleron, Will, I-61-4

Smelcer, Jacob, I-74-2

Smith, Anderson, I-16-2

Smith, D., XII-90-2

Smith, David, I-81-2

Smith, Edward, I-9-4

Smith, John, I-4-2; I-9-4 (2); I-10-2; I-73-4 (2); V-93-4; XII-74-4

Smith, Nich's, I-9-4

Smith, Samuel, I-2-2; V-93-2

Smith, Will, I-24-2; I-81-4 (2); I-82-4

Smith, William, I-82-2 (2)

Smith, Zach'a, I-1-4

Smith, Zebulon, I-77-2 (4); I-82-4

Sneed, Dudley, V-98-4

Solohan, Jno., I-34-4

Somerlin, Winburn, V-97-2

Sparkes, Matt'w, V-107-4

Sparks, Leonard, I-34-4

Sparks, Sam'l, I-19-4

Spaw, Hy., XII-73-4

Starling, David, I-15-2

Steel, David, XII-7-2

Steel, Ninian, I-17-2

Stell, William, I-4-4

Stephenson, John, I-4-4

Stewart, David, I-59-4 (2); XII-16-4

Stewart, James, I-15-4 (2)

Stewart, Jos., I-63-4

Stewart, Robert, I-5-4 (2); I-62-2

Stewart, Will, I-36-4

Stinson, James, I-16-2; I-17-2; I-21-3; I-27-2; I-28-2

Stinson, Jas., I-16-4

Stinson, Robert, I-82-2

Stovall, B., XII-89-4

Stovall, Bartho., I-15-2

Stockdon, Will, I-59-2

Stockton, W., I-47-2

Stockton, Will, I-47-4; I-52-2

Stone, John, I-15-4

Stone, Robert, I-23-4

Stringer, Will, XII-18-4

Stuart, David, I-28-4

Stuart, Thomas, XII-7-2

Sullivan, John, I-7-4

Sullivan, Sam'l, I-5-2; I-51-2

Sulsion, Jacob, I-65-4

Swaggerty, Adam, I-10-4

Sweetin, Edward, I-30-2

Sweeton, Edward, I-24-2

Talbot, Tho., I-47-2; I-56-4

Tarbert, James, I-27-4

Tate, Robert, I-10-2

Tate, Samuel, I-72-4

Taylor, Andrew, V-92-4

Taylor, And'w, I-4-4; I-5-4

Taylor, C., XII-89-4 (2)

Taylor, Chas., I-47-2

Taylor, Charles, I-62-4

Taylor, Chris'r, I-16-2

Taylor, Geo., I-5-2 (2); XII-16-4

Taylor, Isaac, I-4-4; I-65-4; V-93-2 (2)

Teasly, Silas, I-3-4

Tedlock, Joshua, V-93-2

Temple, Major, I-4-4

Terrill, Smith, I-34-4

Terry, Jeptha, I-4-2

Terry, Howel, I-19-4

Tetter, Henry, I-41-2

Thomas, Isaac, I-23-4; I-74-4

Thomas, Ellis, I-59-4

Thomas, Will, I-13-4

Thomas, Wm., I-5-4

Thompson, J., XII-74-2

Thompson, Jacob, I-2-2; I-19-4

Thompson, Sam, I-21-4

Thompson, Samuel, I-79-4

Tiller, Henry, I-11-2

Tipton, Joseph, I-81-4; I-82-2

Tolbert Matt., I-56-4

Tolbert, Matthew, I-48-2

Tolbert, Thomas, I-11-2

Tolbert, Will, I-12-4

Torbet, James, I-41-2

Tounson, Thomas, I-2-4

Travilland, Joab, V-92-4

Travilland, Richard, I-67-4

Travillan, Richard, I-63-2

Trevillian, Richard, I-27-4

Trewillion, Richard, I-5-2

Trimble, Jno., I-4-2

Trimble, John, I-5-2; I-63-2; I-72-4

Trimble, Moses, I-10-2

Trimble, Will, I-20-2; I-63-2 (3); I-63-4

Trimble, Wm., I-11-2; XII-16-4

Tully, Michael, I-4-2

Tully W., XII-89-4

Tunley, Geo., I-7-2

Tunnell, Will, I-72-4

Turbott, James, I-21-2 I-21-4

Turner, Henry, I-13-4

Turner, John, I-1-4

Turner, Reubin, I-7-2

Turney, Henry, I-14-2; I-62-2; I-67-2

Turney, Peter, I-55-4; I-58-2; I-62-2 (3)

Tye, John, I-17-4

Tyhe, John, XII-16-4

Vance, Davis, I-12-4

Vance, Jacob, I-34-4

Vance, John, I-2-4 (2)

Vanhoser, John, I-74-4; I-82-2

Vann, John, I-27-4

Veach, Elijah, I-17-2 (2); I-23-4; I-67-2

Vienable, David, V-93-2

Vermillion, Jessee, I-3-2; I-9-4; I-20-2; I-41-2

Waddle, John, I-13-4; I-67-2

Walden, William, I-80-2

Waldrop, Isaiah, I-21-4

Waldrop, James, I-21-4

Waldrop, Joe, XII-14-2

Waldrop, John, I-60-4

Walker, David, XII-20-2

Walker, Edmund, I-1-4

Wallace, John, I-3-2

Wallace, Thomas, I-1-2

Wallin, Stephen, I-13-4; I-14-2

Wallin, Thomas, I-1-2

Wallin, Will, I-13-4

Walter, Stephen, I-67-2

Ward, James, I-10-2

Ward, John, I-19-4; I-20-2

Warin, Edmund, I-14-2

Waters, Richard, I-28-2

Watson, John, V-97-2

Watson, Jona, I-7-4

Weathers, Jesse, I-16-2; V-98-4

Weaver, Chris'r, I-6-4

Weaver, Fred'k, I-24-2

Weaver, John, I-82-4

Weaver, Sam'l, I-57-2; I-82-2

Weaver, Samuel, I-82-4

Webb, Benjamin, V-93-2

Webb, Geo., I-90-2

Webb, John, I-14-2; I-24-2; I-65-4; I-67-2

Webb, Martin, I-16-2

Webb, Moses, I-24-2

Webb, Sam, I-24-2

Wellhight, Soloman, I-3-2

Wells, Will, I-9-4

Whealock, John, I-10-4

Wheeler, Ambrose, I-1-2; I-52-2

Wheeler, Will, I-60-4

Wheeler, William, I-1-2; I-77-2

White, John, I-11-2

White, Jonas, I-74-2

White, Richard, I-1-2

White, Thomas, I-3-4 (2); I-36-4; XII-7-2

Whitenberger, Henry, I-9-4

Whitson, James, I-3-4 (2); I-4-2

Whitson, Jesse, I-3-4 (2)
Wier, Sam'l, I-60-2 (2)
Wilder, Joab, I-9-4
Williams, Charles, I-71-2
Williams, Edward, I-65-4
Williams, James, I-14-2 (3)
Williams, Jos'a, I-63-2; I-2-2
Williams, Joshua, I-65-4
Williams, Moses, I-16-4
Williams, Sam, I-4-4; I-16-2; I-27-4
Williams, Sam'l, I-20-2
Williams, Thomas, I-34-4; I-73-2
Williams, Wm., V-96-4
Willson, Andrew, I-63-2
Wilson, Adam, I-23-4; I-48-4 (2)
Wilson, Andrew, I-82-2
Wilson, James, I-21-2; I-61-2;
    V-92-4
Wilson, John, I-62-2; V-96-4 (2);
    XII-3-2
Wilson, Joseph, I-14-2; V-103-2
Wilson, Robert, V-96-4; V-98-4 (2)
Wilson, Sam'l, I-9-4
Wilson, Will, V-96-4
Wilson, William, XII-3-2
Wilson, Wm., I-13-4; V-98-4
Wincent, Thomas, I-61-4
Wisner, Lewis, I-15-2
Witt, Elijah, I-51-2
Wittenbarger, Jos., I-13-4
Wittier, Jessee, I-34-4
Witts, Robert, I-79-2

Wood, Absolam, I-48-4
Wood, Absolom, I-24-4
Woodruff, Jesse, V-103-2
Wood, John, I-5-4
Woods, Ann, I-15-2
Woods, John, I-3-2; I-73-4
Woods, Michael, I-17-2
Woods, Mich'l, I-63-2
Woods, Rich., I-9-4
Woods, Richard, I-11-4
Woods, Thomas, I-2-2; I-17-4
Woodward, Sam, I-38-2
Woodward, Thomas, I-11-2; V-97-2
Wray, James, I-3-2; I-44-2
Wright, Benjamin, XII-21-2
Wright, Robert, I-81-4
Wringelling, Chris'r, XII-18-4
Wrogan, Wm., I-90-2
Wyate, James, I-72-4
Wyatt, James, I-9-2
Wyatt, Samuel, I-9-2
Wyatt, Will, I-73-2
Wyatt, William, I-8-2; XII-3-2
Wyet, Sam, I-59-4
Yerby, Isam, I-17-2
York, Will, I-36-4
Young, Charles, I-2-2
Young, John, I-41-2 (2)
Young, Robert, I-2-2 (2); I-3-2
Young, Will, I-30-2
Young, Wm., I-67-2

REVOLUTIONARY PENSION RECORDS

Complete List of Revolutionary Pensioners residing in Tennessee who have received the Benefits of Congress—Act of May 15, 1828.

NAME	COUNTY	RANK	AN. ALLOW.	SERVICE	DATE OF ENROLL.
Thomas Drake	Bedford	P.	£80	Reg. Va. Line	Feb. 2, 1829
Edward King	Bedford	P.	£80	Reg. N. C. Line	Feb. 2, 1829
John Meaderis	Bedford	Capt.	£480	5th Reg. N. C. Line	Feb. 12, 1829
John Townsend	Carroll	Serj.	£180	Washington's Cav.	Nov. 29, 1828
Lipscomb Norvell	Davidson	Lieut.	£320	3rd Reg. Va. Line	Aug. 2, 1828
Benjamin Darrow	Dickson	P.	£80	1st Reg. Ct. Line	Jan. 2, 1829
Daniel Williams	Dickson	Capt.	£480	6th Reb. N. C. Line	Jan. 24, 1829
Benjamin Starritt	Fayette	Dragoon	£100	Lee's Legion	Apr. 26, 1830
John Nelson	Franklin	Maj.	£600	4th Reg. N.C.Line	Dec. 10, 1828
				dropped as fraudulent	
Joseph Britton	Hawkins	Lieut.	£320	Gist's Md. Reg.	Sept. 3, 1828
William Perkins	Hawkins	P.	£80	Hazen's Reg.	Apr. 22, 1829
Robert McKinley	Jackson	P.	£80	Reg. N. C. Line	Nov. 18, 1828
James McClister	Jefferson	P.	£80	Stewart's Pa. Reg.	June 18, 1829
Anthony Mullins	Lincoln	Dragoon	£100	Washington's Cav.	Feb. 28, 1829
George Phillips	Monroe	P.	£80	2nd Reg. N.C.Line	May 23, 1829
				died Oct. 24, 1828	
Wm. Higginbotham	Perry	Serj.	£120	2nd Reg. Va. Line	May 23, 1829
John Tally	Perry	Dragoon	£100	Washington's Cav.	Jan. 15, 1830
John Etter	Rutherford	Dragoon	£100	Washington's Cav.	Dec. 10, 1828
William Lytle	Rutherford	Capt.	£480	1st N. C. Line	Sept. 1, 1828
Joseph Newman	Rutherford	P.	£80	Reg. Va. Line	Dec. 18, 1828
James Ramsey	Rutherford	Dragoon	£100	Armand's Corps	Feb. 7, 1829
Thomas Allmond	Stewart	Dragoon	£100	Lee's Legion	Dec. 11, 1828
John T. Turner	Stewart	P.	£80	4th Reg. Md. Line	Nov. 29, 1829
Died April 27, 1831. Mary Turner, widow.					
Joshua Hadley	Sumner	Capt.	£480	Reg. N. C. Line	July 9, 1828
Died February 8, 1830					
John P. Waggoner	Sumner	Lieut.	£320	Reg. Ga. Line	Jan. 3, 1832
Died August 22, 1828					
John Scott	Wilson	Serj.	£120	Reg. N. C. Line	July 1, 1829
Charles Smith	Wilson	Trumpeter	£120	Washington's Cav.	Feb. 16, 1829

WILLS OF WASHINGTON COUNTY, TENNESSEE
County Court Clerk's Office, Jonesboro, Tennessee

Francis, Ephraim, 417
Galleher, James, 23
Gillespie, George, 31
Grisham, Thomas, 64
Gott, Anthony, 90
Grate, David, 139
Gyne, Catrena, 195
Gibson, Thomas, 202
Greer, Samuel, 234
Gates, John, 232
Gore, Christian, 245
Greenway, William C., 261
Glasscock, Sarah, 264
Gibson, Mary, 286
Greene, John, 337
Gott, John, 323
Garber, Michael, 365
Green, Ira, 371
Greenway, Richard, 385
Gibson, Thomas, 414
Greene, Joshua, 426
Glass, Hiram, 440
Gwin, Thomas, 560
Hider, Michael, 21
Hay, Charles, 27
Hampton, Robert, 42
Hendley, James, 47
Hale, George, Sen'r, 67
Hoss, Peter, 94
Harlet, Kinler, 95
Hunt, Simon, 101
Hoss, Jacob, 110
Hammer, John, 113
Hale, Nicholas, 118
Hale, Joseph, 134
Hale, Henry, 135
Hunter, John, Sen'r, 143
Hammer, Margaret, 187
Hale, Elizabeth, 188
Hammer, Jonathan, 189
Hall, James, 216

Hammonds, Thomas, 229
Hail, George, 254
Hammer, Jacob, 259
Hale, Jackson, 256
Hartman, Henry, 267
Harmon, Adam, 335
Harris, John C., 304
Hannah, Andrew, 314
Hale, Joseph, 325
Henley, Isaac, 355
Hale, John, 354
Holt, Jacob, 349
Hodges, Roland, 363
Hannah, Jane, 377
Hale, Canday, 379
Hunter, John Joseph, 394
Halle, Eliza Ann, 397
Hale, Henry, 401
Hunt, Samuel, 411
Hunt, Sarah, 413
Howard, John, 436
Harris, Hugh, 453
Hale, William, 566
Hale, Martha, 570
Hale, Archibald, 449
Irwin, James, 40
Jervis, Alexander, 62
Ingle, Michael, 78
Ingle, William, 93
Job, Abigail, 120
Jenkins, Aaron, 121
Ides, William, 121
Isenberge, Henry, 173
Irwin, Rebecca, 231
Jackson, William, 271
Jordan, Lewis, 364
Jones, Darling, 366
Johnston, James S., 377
Jackson, George, 407
Jackson, Peter, 421
Jones, John, 580

ABSTRACTS OF WILLS—WASHINGTON COUNTY, TENNESSEE

Vol. 1, p. 1—Will of Rebecca Vanderpool, May 12, 1799.
To Peter Nave, husband of d. Ann. Son Abraham Vanderpool.
Ex. Peter Nave.
Thomas Houghton, James Grayson, Elizabeth Grayson, Teste.
Proven August Sessions, 1779.

P. 1—Will of Joab Mitchell, Oct. 27, 1779:
Wife—Mary Mitchell, sole heir.
Teste: John Coulter, Richard Mitchell, Jane X. Coulter.
Recorded May Sessions, 1780.

P. 2—Will of Nathaniel Davis, "of Washington County, State of North Carolina," Feb. 21, 1781:
Bro. Robert Davis; Mother; Sisters Mary, Ann, Elizabeth.
Bro. Robert's sons. James. Bros. Robert and Isaac, Exs.
Teste: Robert Davis, Mary Davis.
Recorded May Sessions, 1781.

P. 2—Will of Aaron Burleson, Nov. 16, 1781.
Wife; Sons, John, Jonathan, Joseph; d. Elizabeth; s. Thomas; d. Sarah; s. Aaron; ds. Rachel, Nancy, Abigail, Mary, Rhoda. Wife and son Aaron, Exs.
Teste: Thomas Williams, Patrick X Shields, Henry Clark.
Recorded May Sessions, 1782.

P. 3—Will of John Paveley (written Pables in body of will), April 12, 1781, "of Chucky, in County of Washington".
Yoeman: wife, Elizabeth; s. William; s. Elijah; s. James; ds. Mary, Frances, Lucia, Elizabeth, Eysa, Margaret.
Eldest son, Lewis.
Teste: George Mooney, Charles X. Dotson, John Powers, Jonathan Currier.
Recorded May Sessions, 1782.

P. 4—Will of William Beane:
Wife Liddy, negro girl "Grace," horses, cattle, household goods, land and mill during her natural life, at her decease to son Russell. Remainder of estate to be divided amongst my surviving children.
Sons William, Robert and George, Executors.
Teste: Thomas Hardeman, John X Callihan, Robert Stone.
May Sessions.

P. 5—Will of Adam Broyles.

April 19, 1782. Eldest son, Moses; ss. Aaron and Joshua; d. Milla Panther; Mima Broyles. Negroes and Kentucky lands; d—Anne Brown; Friends Joseph Brown, Moses Broyles and William Moore.
Teste: John X Waddle, Coonrod Willpightle, Mathias Broyles.
May Sessions, 1782.

P. 6—Will of John Nodding, Nov. 6, 1782:
Wife, Priscilla—Slaves and land.
Teste: Samuel Wood, James Scott.
February Sessions, 1783.

P. 6—Will of Peter Kuykendall, Feb. 17, 1783:
Son, Jesse slave and land; d. Jane; s. Adam; d. Elizabeth; s. Matthew; s. Peter; ch. Mary, Ruthy, Rebecca, Offay.
Brother, Abraham, executor.
Teste: Andrew Thompson, John Kuykendall, Robert Irwin.
May Sessions, 1783.

P. 7—Will of Baptist McNabb:
Jan. 4, 1784, "Washington County, North Carolina." d. Isabella McNabb; ss. John, David, Jonathan; ds. Mary, Margaret, Jane, Ketrin. Sons John and David, executors.
Teste: Wm. McNabb, Agness Campbell, John Campbell.
May Sessions, 1784.

P. 8—Will of Thomas Mitchell:
North Carolina, Washington County, June 14, 1784.
d. Margaret McAdow; s. James; d. Elizabeth Thompson; s. Thomas; d. Sarah Mitchell.
Teste: Robert Irwin, Mary Irwin.
August Sessions, 1784.

P. 9—Will of Randolph Crecelias:
Jan. 7, 1787. Wife, Elizabeth; ss. Isaac, John, Jacob. Ch. John, Elizabeth, Barberry, Catherine, Isaac, Dolly, Margaret, Jacob.
Teste: James Cash, Abraham Riffe, Philip X Coussions.
November Sessions, 1787.

P. 10—Will of Andrew Taylor:
May 22nd, 1787, "ch. Washington County, State of North Carolina."
Wife, Ann; sons Isaac, David McNabb, Andrew Taylor, Nathaniel

Taylor; Matthew; "till youngest child Rhoda comes of age."   d. Rebecca, slaves to each child.

Teste: John Hyder, William English.

November Session, 1787.

P. 12—Will of John Fain:

July 15, 1788.   Wife, Agnes, sons to share equally.   d. Ruth Fain negro "Punch."

Teste: Rosannah X Fain.

November Sessions, 1788.

P. 12—Will of John Bullard:

Oct. 15, 1780, wife, Mary Bullard.

Teste: Joseph X Nation, Elinor X Nation, Ann X Bullard.

November Sessions, 1780.

P. 13.   Will of John Cox:

Oct. 19, 1777.   sons, Abraham and William two negroes;   ds. Jane and Agnes; "slaves I should have had from my father's estate."   Abraham and William Cox and John Sevier, Exs.

Teste: John Carter, Christopher Cunningham, Emanuel Carter.

No date of probate.

P. 13—Will of Christopher Cunningham:

Nov. 10, 1782.   Wife Mary; my fifteen children: Elizabeth Gatril, Susannah Robertson, Lyddia Cunningham, John Cunningham, Mary Job, Ann Orr, Sarah Cunningham, Jane Cunningham, Jacob, Joseph, Matthew, Moses, Aaron, Elinor, David.

Ds. Elizabeth Gatril and Susannah Robertson to have no part in legacy that John Musgrove left Mary, my wife.   "Till youngest child come of age."

Mathew Talbot and Joseph Tipton, Exs.

Teste: Robert Orr, Isaac Taylor.

May Sessions, 1783.

P. 15—Will of Robert Fowler:

Sept. 22, 1784.   Mother, Ann Fowler; child Esther Fowler.

Exs. William Fowler and Wife Agnes Fowler.

Teste: Abed'o. Inman, Adam Willson, Molly Inman.

August Sessions, 1785.

P. 15—Will of Thomas Dillard:

May 13, 1784.   Wife one half of slaves.   Ch. Benjamin, Winnesophia,

Mary Ann, Thomas, Stacy, Martha, Amy, John, Rebecca; d. Elizabeth Huchings; d. Mary Ann Love; d. Stacy.

Wife Martha and son-in-law Robert Love, Exs.

Robert Love guardian for minor children, Sept. 23, 1784.

Teste: Edmond Samms, John Samms, John Webb.

———— Sessions, 178-.

P. 17—Will of William Carson:

March 10, 1790. Wife Margaret, Oldest d. Jennet; d. Mary; oldest s. William; s. John.

David Carson, John Strain, Exs.

May Sessions, 1790.

P. 18—Will of John Potter:

Nov. 18, 1789. Washington County, North Carolina.

Wife, Hannah; ss. John, Johnston; s-in-l Adam Rainbolt; s. Abraham; ch. Nancy, John, Elizabeth, Johnston, Sarah. Wife Hannah and friends Cornelius Bowman and Thomas Whelson, Exs.

Teste: William Moreland, John X Grindstaff, Isaac Grindstaff.

May Sessions, 1790.

P. 19—Will of Walter Bayley:

June 10, 1790. Washington County, North Carolina.

Wife—land in Sussex County, Virginia, in care of Thomas Whitfield. Slaves to daughters Mary and Lucy, and Wife. To Sarah Maggot, d. of Mary Maggot, land in Sussex Co., Va. Joseph Greer, of Washington Co., N. C., and Etheldred Davis, of Sussex Co., Va., Exs.

Teste: Thomas Reneau, Archer Evans, Charlot Evans.

August Sessions, 1790.

P. 20—Will of David Matlock:

March 15, 1790, Washington County, N. C. Three ds. Sarah, Elizabeth, Catherine. Wife Margaret. Sons George, David, Gideon. S. David and Joseph Greer, Exs.

Teste: Moses Humphreys, Peter Parkson, And'w. X Sholdy.

August Sessions, 1790.

P. 21—Will of Michael Hider:

May 28, 1790. Wife Elizabeth; sons John, Michael, Adam, Jacob, Joseph. Wife and s. John, Exs.

Teste: Edm'd. Williams, Robert English, Henry X English.

August Sessions, 1790.

P. 22—Will of Benjamin Blackburn.

August 10, 1786. "of the State of Franklin and county of Washington, farmer."

Wife Mary "good sufficient genteel and handsome maintaince during her life of all things necessary." To son Benjamin "my Great Bible;" to each grandson named Benjamin "a good school Bible." To son John's son Samuel. d. Ann; d. Elizabeth Bay. Archibald's bond to Thomas Bay. s. Archibald and John Wear, Exs.

Teste: James Cunningham, Jeremiah Robinson, Andrew Hannah.
August Sessions, 1791.

P. 23—Will of James Galleher:

Sept. 22, 1791. Washington County of the Western Waters.

Wife, Sarah, George, Thomas, James "having got their share." Young-est son David, s. John.

Teste: George Gillespie, John Allison, Robert McFarland.
February Sessions, 1792.

P. 23—Will of Robert Young:

"County of Washington, Territory of the United States of America, South of the Ohio River." Wife, Mary; s. Joseph; d. Elizabeth Gilla-land; d. Martha Cashedy; ch. John, William, Robert, Thomas, Charles, Joseph; ds. Sarah Long, Margaret Bates; Mary Dugless; Agnes Henry; grandsons Joseph Young s. of deceased son James, Robert Gillaland and Cashedy. Wife Mary and s. Joseph. Exs. February 7, 1792.

Teste: Thomas Gourley, James Gunnon, Absolem Scott.
May Sessions, 1792.

P. 25. Will of Thomas Bell.

March 19, 1792. Wife Elizabeth; ss. John and David. ds. Sarah and Mary. Wife Elizabeth and brother William Bell, Exs.

Teste: Robert Carson, James Bell.
May Sessions, 1792.

P. 26—Will of Robert Allison:

April 26, 1792. "Washington County, Territory in the United States of America, South of the Ohio River." Wife Ann; two youngest ds. Jane and Polly; d. Ann; youngest s. Robert. "My married children."

Teste: John Anderson, George Bell.
May Sessions, 1792.

P. 27—Will of William Shealds:

Feb. 10, 1791. Wife. s. Joseph, Rest of Children equally. s. Joseph and Andrew Thompson, Exs.

Teste: John Campbell, David Brown, Robert Bleakly.
November Sessions, 1792.

P. 27—Will of Charles Hay:
December 23rd, 1792.   "of Washington County in the Ceded Territory
Southwest of the Ohio River."   Wife, Rebecca; household goods and
the following books—her Bible, Boston Fourfold State of Man, Erskin's
Gospel Sonnets, a book entitled A Dead Faith Anatornized.   To nephew
Charles Grier, my dictionary with an old book of Arithmetic.   To nephew
Charles Hatcher, 2nd volume of Baxter's Philosophical Inquiry in the Na-
ture of the Human Solel.   To sister Hulda Grier the 4th Volume of Dr.
Doddridge's Family Expository.   To sister Sarah Hatcher's daughter
Anna 2nd volume of Family Expository.   To Charles H. Nelson my wife's
sister's son ten dollars.   To brother Reuben Hay.   To Wife's sister Sarah
Robinson one new Bible.   To sister Hulda Grier's youngest d. Mary
Grier.   To Jamiston Hatcher's youngest ds. Sarah and Rebecca.   To
Harris Hatcher, son of James Hatcher.   To Charles Hatcher and James
Hatcher sons of Jameson Hatcher. $195 of estate of James Grier, dec'd.,
put to interest May 19, 1779.   Wife Rebecca, Capt. James Scott, Nathaniel
Davis, Exs.
   Teste: Henry McMullen, Agness X Davis, Mary McMullen.
   February Sessions, 1793.

P. 29—Will of William Noding, Jun'r:
Sept. 15, 1792.   Nephew Charles McCray.   To Sister Elizabeth Cal-
vert negro "Adam."   To nephews Charles McCray and John Calvert
land on Camp creek if my father William Noding obtains a deed for it.
Sisters Sarah McCray, Mary Bayles, Elinor Hill and Alis Brown's, dec'd.,
children Mill seat where bro. John Noding lived.   Daniel McCray and
William Calvert, Exs.
   Teste: Samuel Wood, Sen'r. James Wood, Samuel Wood, Jun'r.
   May Sessions, 1793.

P. 30—Will of Joseph Barron:
Territory South of Ohio, Washington County, Aug. 2, 1793.   Wife
Ann, Five ch. John, Joseph, William, Henry, James.   ds. Sarah Dotson,
Mary Ford, Walker Barron.   Sons Joseph and William, Exs.
   Teste: John Kinchloe, Margaret X Barron.
   August Sessions, 1793.

P. 31—Will of Joseph Trotter:
January 8, 1794.   Wife Jenny; bros. Alexander and James.   "Chest
at Col. Roddie's."

Teste: John Carmicle, Isabella Trotter, Margaret Carmicle.
February Sessions, 1794.

P. 31—Will of George Gillespie:
December 14, 1794. "of Green County, Territory South of Ohio river." Wife, Martha; to s. Thomas and his s. George; d. Martha Jack and her s. George Jack; d. Jane Gillespie; s. John; d. Elizabeth Hays and her s. Charles Hays; to g s. George Gillespie s. of John; Three sons George, Allen, James. Slaves to each. Wife & Sons George and Allen, Exs.
Teste: F. A. Ramsey, George Galleher, Henry Earnest.
February Sessions, 1794.

P. 33—Will of Samuel Shaw:
"of Washington County in the ceded Territory." July 29, 1794. Wife Margaret, sons Francis and Samuel. Married daughters.
Teste: Margaret Spear, Samuel Brison, Wm. Purselly.
November Sessions, 1794.

P. 34—Will of James Allison:
September 21, 1794. Wife Jane. To Elizabeth Scott, Hannah Scott, Rachel Sharp, Esther Allison; To d. Elizabeth Allison. Robert Allison, Nathaniel Davis, James Chastin, Exs.
Teste: Frank X Allison, John Adams, Michael Harrison.
May Sessions, 1795.

P. 34—Will of Isaac Denton:
July 14, 1795. Sons Isaac and Jeremiah Denton. Wife Ann; ds. Martha, Agge and Elizabeth Denton. Susanna Rider.
Teste: Jesse Whitson, David Job.
May Sessions, 1795.

P. 35—Will of Alexander Trotter:
April 24, 1795. Wife, Isabella, Sons, David and Joseph. d. Susanna. Wife Isabella and James Carmicle, Sen'r, Exs.
Teste: Alexander Stuart, Abigail Carmicle.
November Sessions, 1795.

P. 36—Will of Edmund Williams:
Territory of United States, Washington County, Sept. 16, 1795.
Wife Lucretia, sons Joshua, Samuel, George and Archibald. d. Levina Tipton; d. Terphena Williams, d. Sarah Adams Williams; s. John Lindsey Williams; son Joshua Williams of Bomcomb Co., N. C., and son Archibald Williams of Washington Co., Exs.

Teste: Wm. Davis, Chas. Whitson, Wm. Whitson.
November Sessions, 1795.

P. 38—Will of Joshua Wood:
June 11, 1773. Wife Agnes; s. John Wood; d. Wineford Wood;
ds. Milly and Elizabeth Wood; d. Agnes Wood; s. Richard; s. Elijah;
s. Henry.
Robert Donald and William Armstrong, exs.
Teste: Robert Ewing, Robert Irwin, Barbary X Mayberry.

P. 39—Will of William Whitson:
October 16, 1783, "of Washington County, State of North Carolina."
To son Jesse Whitson whole estate.   ds. Susannah Eajan and Lydda
McKay. sons Joseph and Jesse, Exs.
Teste: Henry Nelson, Jun'r; William Wood, Reubin Rider.
November Sessions, 1783.

P. 40—Will of James Irwin:
Wife Mary; s. Benjamin; s. Robert; ds. Lettice, Ellenor, Mary, Eliza.
To Ellnor's child Rose; account against Neil McFall whose estate is in
the hands of William Duffle in Pennsylvania.
Teste: Richard Jones, Samuel X King.
February Sessions, 1796.

P. 41—Will of George Kindal:
November 18, 1795. Wife Barbary and children.
Teste: Samuel Wood, Martin Sidner, Michael Harmon.
February Sessions, 1796.

P. 41—Will of John White:
"of Washington County in the territory of the United States South
of the river Ohio (alias Tennessee)."   May 14, 1796. Wife Ann.   Children as they come of age.
Teste: Joseph Brittin, John X Hill, Ellinor Hill.
May Sessions, 1796.

P. 42—Will of Robert Hampton:
March 29, 1796. Wife Mary; oldest son John; s. George; s. Robert;
s. William; s. Jesse.
Teste: Reubin Bayles, Mary X Eton.
August Sessions, 1796.

P. 42—Will of James Boren:
October 14, 1795. Wife Sarah; s. William; s. John Dopon Boren;

s. Absolem; s. Chaney; s. James. d. Rachel Price, wife of Mordiciai Price; d. Abrrodla Moore; d. Tempereace Boren; d. Martha Ball; d. Frances Downing.

Teste: Horatio Ford, Edward X Smith.

August Sessions, 1796.

P. 44—Will of Charles Robertson, Sen'r:

"of County of Washington, State of Tennessee." Aug. 31, 1798.

Wife Susannah; sons and daughters; to s. William negro "Kate;" To Rosamond Beane negro "Rhoda." To Kesiah Sevier "a likely negro girl." To Sarah Cox $10. Real estate 2000 acres lying at Mussel Shoals to be taken out of 8000 acre tract, 1000 a. to James Gordan and 1000 a. to Charles Sevier.

Teste: Henry Taylor, Abraham Hartsell, Ears. Witt.

Charles Robertson, Jun'r, and James Gordan qualified as Executors.

November Sessions, 1798.

P. 44—Will of Samuel Culbertson.

"of Washington County, State of Tennessee." December 24, 1798.

Wife Jane; ch. Andrew, Josiah, Samuel, Joseph, James, Mary and Weakfield. Wife, Robert Love and Daniel McCray, Exs.

Teste: James Deakins, John Young, Holland Hyggins.

February Sessions, 1799.

P. 45—Will of John Carmicle:

February 27, 1799. Wife, Isabella 1-2 of plantation; s. James; Mary Moore, my oldest daughter £5; d. Margaret Carmicle; d. Jenny. Sons George Pumry and Archibald to devide land in Grassy Vally, George to have improvements on part next to Knoxville. To sons John and Daniel plantation on Tennessee river. To son David home plantation after wife's decease. To son William the mill. Youngest d. Elizabeth. David Thompson and wife, Isabella, Executors.

Teste: Peter Smetzer, John Adam.

Isabella Carmicle and Andrew Thompson qualified as Exs.

May Sessions, 1799.

P. 46—Will of Liles Brooks:

February 17, 1799. Wife Jane. Children as they come of age. Wife and John Bayles, Exs.

Teste: Daniel Bayles, Colvin Finch, Ann Bayles.

May Sessions, 1799.

P. 46—Will of James Henley:

s. John heir to my land and livery. Wife. Father.

Teste: John Hendley, Caty Hendley.
May Sessions, 1799.

P. 47—Will of Charles Longmire:
Oct. 28, 1797; codicil July 17th, 1799.   s. John; s. William; s. Joseph;
s. George.   d. Sarah Longmire; other children.
Teste: Peter Brown, John Brown.
November Sessions, 1799.

P. 49—Will of Jonathan Watson:
Oct. 15, 1796.   Wife, Martha and Children.   Wife and Major John
Sevier, Exs.
Teste: Samuel Wood, David Smith, Wm. Wood.
November Sessions, 1799.

P. 50—Will of Johnson Whitaker:
Oct. 24, 1799.   Wife Sarah and Children.
Teste: Mark Whitaker, Jonathan Tullis.
February Sessions, 1800.

P. 50—Will of James Caruthers:
February 13, 1799.   To d. Jane Smith "all my books" and a legacy
willed to her mother by her grandfather.   Richard Smith, Ex.
Teste: John Bleakley, John McCall, Jane McCall.
February Sessions, 1800.

P. 51—Will of Will Watson:
March 9, 1800.   Wife Nancy, s. William; s. Jonathan; d. Mary;
d. Elizabeth; d. Susannah land adjoining Robert Young; ds. Hannah and
Abigail.   Wife, Joseph Young and Jonathan Tullis, Exs.
Teste: John Parker, Thomas Linville, Robert X Cashedy.
May Sessions, 1800.

P. 51—Will of Samuel Wood, Sen'r:
April 26, 1800.   Wife Sarah; eldest son William; s. James; s. Samuel;
s. Thomas; s. Abraham; s. John; s. George; d. Mary Hendricks.   Wife
and sons Abraham and John, Exs.
Teste: Wm. Carlvert, Martin Sidner, Colvin Finch.
August Sessions, 1800.

P. 52—Will of William Daniel:
May 23, 1794.   Wife Ann; Two sons John and William; Five daugh-

ters, Mary, Ann, Phebe, Jemima and Alice Daniel. Friend Joseph Crouch, Ex.

Teste: David Job, Philemon Lacy.

August Sessions, 1800.

P. 53—Will of Samuel Sherrill.

June 4, 1800. Daughter Catherine Sevier, wife of John Sevier, Sen'r, "a negro wench named Rachel and her youngest child about ten weeks old." Sons Uriah and John Sherrill; d. Mary Jones wife of Littlepage Simons two slaves; sons George and William "land on which I now live being 200 acres purchased from John Sevier on Nolachucky river adjoining land of John Sevier." son Adam.

John Sevier, Sen'r, and William Sherrill, Exs.

Teste: Benjamin Were, George Were.

August Sessions, 1800.

P. 54—Will of John Weir:

January 7, 1800. Wife Agnes; 3 youngest daughters Nancy, Phebe and Susannah; 2 ds. Betsy and Jane; sons Benjamin, George, Hugh when he comes of age, John; d. Mary Cunningham; d. Margaret Wilson. Wife Agnes, s. Benjamin and s-in-l John Wilson, Exs.

Teste: John Nelson, Reubin Payne, Allen Mathis.

August Sessions, 1800.

P. 55—Will of Thomas Rodgers.

April 10, 1800. Son Samuel "mansion house and plantation adjoining where Andrew Rodgers now lives;" s. William; s. Andrew land to Joseph Metcalf's line. Three girls. Sons Moses and James Rodgers, Exs.

Teste: Jas. Rogers, Thos. Biddle.

August Sessions, 1800.

P. 56—Will of James Martin:

January 6, 1801. Wife and Children. Samuel Denton, Ex.

Teste: Jonathan Mulkey, John Carr, Jun'r, Joseph Britten.

February Sessions, 1801.

P. 57—Will of Henry Stevens:

January 10, 1801. Wife Margaret; stepson James Barnes; sons David and Isaac Stevens. step ds. Jenny, Polly and Peggy Barnes and Nancy, William, Betsy, Thomas, John and Henry Stevens to share equally. Wife Margaret and Wm. Ward, Exs.

Teste: Henry King, James Morrison, James Barnes.

May Sessions, 1801.

P. 58. Will of Fredrick Sanders:
June 10, 1801. Wife Margaret, s. Frederick "What doctor's drugs are on hand to be sold." Jacob Simmerly, of Washington Co., Virginia, sole Ex.
Teste: J. Brittin, Thomas Enson.
August Sessions, 1801.

P. 59—Will of Robert Blair:
April 6, 1801. Wife Jean; ch. Mary, John, Martha, Anna, Isabel and David "until they are of age," James Buoin, my boy to stay with them. All to be schooled. Friend Robert Allison and bros. John and William, Exs.
Teste: Brue Blair, Alexander McLin, John Cunningham.
February Sessions, 1802.

P. 59—Will of Adam Mitchell:
April 3, 1802. Wife, Elizabeth; d. Margaret; s. John land adjoining John Fair; s. Robert; s. William land in Guilford Co., N. C.; s. Adam land purchased of James Witherspoon; To sons Samuel, David, James and Hezekiah remaining lands. ds. Ibby, Rebecca, Jenny.
Teste: Nicholas Fair, John Hammer.
August Sessions, 1802.

P. 60—Will of Benjamin Shipley:
April 2, 1802. Wife Elizabeth; s. Nathan; g. d. Rebecca d. of son Nathan. s. James. "all my children."
Teste: Joseph Brittin, James Chamberlain.
February Sessions, 1803.

P. 61—Will of James Sehorne:
March 1, 1803. Wife two daughters and two sons. Samuel Davis, Ex.
Teste: James McWherter, Polly Reaney McWhorter.
May Sessions, 1803.

P. 62—Will of Alexander Jervis:
April 10, 1803. Wife Ellenor. To Iseac McInturff for use of his oldest son; To George Clouse Sen'r, for his son Jacob. To d. Rebeccah; To d. Ellinor. Wife and son William Jarvis, Exs.
Teste: Aaron X Clouse, Joel X Parker, R. Love.
August Sessions, 1803.

P. 62—Will of John Blair:
September 17, 1803. Wife Jenny Blair. Adopted son James Moore. Bros. James and Samuel Blair, Exs.

Teste: John Strain, James Tweddy.
November Sessions, 1803.

P. 63—Will of Jesse Clark:
October 5, 1801.   Wife and Children.
Teste: James Sevier, Thomas Brown, Mary Clark.
November Sessions, 1803.

P. 64—Will of William Carson:
January 21, 1804.   Wife Polly, ch. Susanna, Ann, Robert, William,
Polly.   "When William comes of age."   Wife, Polly Carson, David
Wilson and Samuel Davis, Exs.
Teste: Ellenor X Humphrey, Wm. Caruthers, Jenny Caruthers.
February Sessions, 1804.

P. 65—Will of Joseph Booth:
December 30, 1804.   Wife Sarah; s. Joseph; s. John; s. David; ds.
Elizabeth, Jemima; Phebe, Rachel, Sarah and Jane.   Son David, s-in-l
John Million and Eli Edwards, Exs.
Teste: Isaac Hair, Iasaac Ember, Elihu Embree.
May Sessions, 1805.

P. 66—Will of Thomas Murrey:
Sept. 5, 1802.   Grandson Thomas Murrey, son of son Shadrack; gs.
Jabez Murrey, s. of s. Thomas; d. Elizabeth Philips; d. Uroth King; d.
Ann Doty, wife of Joseph Doty; d. Mary Barron, wife of William Barron;
d. Sarah Barron, wife of Joseph Barron; sons Christopher, Shadrack and
Thomas.
Teste: Joseph Brittin, Enoch Kinchloe, Jemima X Kinchloe.
May Sessions, 1805.

P. 67—Will of George Hale, Sen'r:
April 30, 1805.   Wife, Anne; granddaughter Susannah, d. of s. George
Hale; s. Samuel, d. Elizabeth; d. Ann; s. George; "all my Children."
Teste: Nicholas Hale, Sen'r, Jesse Crouch.
August Sessions, 1805.

P. 68—Will of Catherine Robertson.
July 27, 1796.   "of Sullivan County, State of Tennessee."
"only son Jacob Robinson."
Teste: John Chester, Daniel Duff.
November Sessions, 1805.

P. 69—Will of Robert Young:
October 19, 1804.   Wife Phebe; ss. James, Jonathan, Thomas, Joseph,

Robert. Wife and Jonathan Duglas, Exs. s. William 100 a. on Harpeth in Williamson Co.; s. John land in Williamson Co. Three young daughters.

Teste: Wm. Young, Abraham Job, Joshua Job.
May Sessions, 1806.

P. 70—Will of Michael Bricker:
December 21, 1805. Wife, Barbary; d. Betsy Oberboker; d. Christiana Oberboker; ss. John, Michael, Jacob, William. Other children. S. John and Thomas Telford, Exs.
Teste: John Nelson, Jas. Houston, Alex. M. Nelson.
May Sessions, 1806.

P. 70—Will of Alexander Mathis, Sen'r:
June 3, 1806. Wife Anne; s. Ebenezer; s. Alexander "plantation adjoining Mr. Doak, and while there is a college kept at Salem Church he is to allow 50 acres for its use." s. George L.; s. Jeremiah; s. John; d. Grace Patton; d. Rachel Mathis; ch. Miriam Telford, Allen Mathis, Alexander, Jr., George L.; Jeremiah, Grace Patton, Ebenezer L., John and Rachel. Sons Alexander and George, Exs.
Teste: John Nelson, Andrew Hannah, Thomas Telford.
August Sessions, 1806.

P. 72—Will of William Kelsey:
s. John; gd. Agnes Goudy Kelsey; d. Susannah Blair; d. Margaret; Adams; gd. Agnes Adams; gs. William Adams; gd. Nancy Blair; d. Elizabeth Davis; d. Ann McCracken; gd. Agnes Kelsey McCracken; d. Mary Patton; s. John Kelsey and s-in-l John Blair, Exs.
Teste: Henry Nelson, Ann Nelson, Robert Patton.
August Sessions, 1806.

P. 73—Will of Jane Nelson:
November 4, 1799. Deceased husband Henry Nelson. d. Jemima Tyler. Four sons, William, Henry, John and Charles Nelson.
Teste: Adam Lowry, Zadock Willet, Jesse Payne.
February Sessions, 1807.

P. 73—Will of James Cash.
April 10, 1806. Wife, Margaret, Eldest son James; s. John; d. Sally Thomas and her two sons William and Isaac; s. William; s. Leonard; s. Thomas; s. Zachariah; d. Margaret Cash; d. Patsy Anderson; s. Asbury; s. Benjamin. Wife, s. Benjamin and Wm. Colvert, Sen'r, Exs.
"If d. Patsy should die before her husband Ephriam."

Teste: Joseph Keher, Samuel Berryman.
May Sessions, 1807.

P. 74—Will of John Ferguson:
July 29, 1806.   Wife Jane;   s. Samuel;   d. Betsy Hodge;   s. Ester Oar;
Wife and son Samuel, Exs.
Teste: James Kennedy, Joseph Duncan, George Bell.
May Sessions, 1807.

P. 75—Will of John English, Sen'r:
December 20, 1798.   Wife, Agnes;   s. Thomas;   s. John;   Two gss.
John and Thomas sons of son Andrew English, dec'd;   d. Jane English;
d.²Elizabeth English;   d. Sarah Dodridge;   d. Agnes English.
Teste: Isaac White, Thomas Robison, Andrew English.
August Sessions, 1807.

P. 76—Will of John McClure:
January 9, 1808.   Wife;   sons Robert and Ewin;   s. James;   s. William;
ds. Mary and Nancy.   Wm. Bayles, Wm. and John McClure, Exs.
Teste: Wm. Crabtre, Thomas Macy, Sam'l Cloyd.
February Sessions, 1808.

P. 77—Will of Robert Mitchell:
November 7, 1808.   Wife, Elizabeth lots in Jonesboro;   son James;
ds. Jenny and Eliza.   Robert Allison and William Fain, Sen'r, Exs.
Teste: John C. Harris, Sarah Fain, Wm. Robison.
February Sessions, 1809.

P. 78—Will of Michael Inglis:
December 13, 1808.   Wife Mary;   wife's son Jacob Varner;   s. John;
Children.   Alex.   Mathis and Adam Slyger, Exs.
Teste: Abraham Williams, Simon Hart, Adam Inglis.
February Sessions, 1809.

P. 79—Will of William Ellis:
Sept. 11, 1809.   Wife Martha;   d. Margaret Beane and Edmund Beane,
her husband;   s. Jacob;   d. Martha;   s. Clark;   s. Elijah;   ss. James, William
and John;   sons James and Jacob and Daniel Bowman, Exs.
Grand ch. Ellis Grisham, Elizabeth and Margaret Grisham.
Teste: Joseph Brittin, James Crabtree, Michael Crouse.
November Sessions, 1809.

P. 81—Will of Phebe Young:
February 26, 1810.   ds. Phebe and Anna;   sons Joseph and Robert.

Teste: Edward Treewits, James Young.
May Sessions, 1810.

P. 81—Will of Abraham Smith:
June 25, 1810. Wife Martha. Children except Isaac and George who are to have "land they live on in Blount County." ds. Rachel and Hannah. Closson and Isaac Hammer, Exs.
Teste: Thomas and Samuel Stenfield.
August Sessions, 1810.

P. 82—Will of Mary Young:
March 29, 1808. To son James "Jane Davis's part of land I bought that fell to her as legatee of Thomas Young, dec'd." James to pay his son Thomas Young and Thomas Rutledge Davis. d. Polly; s. William; d. Caty; sons Joseph and James. Exs.
Teste: John Parker, Barnet Bowman.
August Sessions, 1810.

P. 82—Will of Joseph Barnes:
November 23, 1810. Wife Mary and children. Wife and Joseph Kenner Exs.
Teste: John White, Jacob Holt.
February Sessions, 1811.

P. 83—Will of Christian White:
May 9, 1810. Wife Elizabeth whole estate.
Teste: William Sands, Christian Zetty.
February Sessions, 1811.

P. 84—Will of John Cosson:
September 24, 1810. Wife Margaret; sons John E. and Isaac N. Cosson; d. Selina Johnston; ds. Delilah, Abbinah, Serinah, Cynthia, Maria and Mercy Cosson.
Wife and sons, Exs.
Teste: John Helm, Sam'l Davis, Henry French.
November Sessions, 1811.

P. 85—Will of Susannah Woodrow:
May 5, 1810. "of Jonesboro, Washington County." land and real estate in city of Philadelphia, daughter Elizabeth Jackson; To David Deaderick, of Jonesboro; to gs. Henry Jackson of Davidson Co.; To James V. Anderson of Jonesboro; d. Elizabeth Jackson wife of Samuel Jackson

and their following ch: Eliza, Caroline, Harriet and Alfred E. Jackson.
Teste: Wm. Roddman, John Adams, Joseph Brown, Hugh Brown.
February Sessions, 1812.

P. 86—Will of James Cox:
November 13, 1810. s. George; two youngest daughters; s. Mayberry
T. Cox; d. Susannah; youngest d. Dorcas; s. James; d. Mary Hale, wife
of Nicholas Hale; s. John; d. Sarah Strong, wife of Obediah Strong; d.
Fanny Hale, wife of Gideon Hale. Jacob Hoss, Sen'r, Joseph Crouch,
Sen'r, and Chas. Daryworth, Exs.
Teste: Peter Hoss, Henry Bowers, Thos. Buckingham.

P. 87—Will of John Cunningham:
March 5, 1812. Wife Martha; s. Samuel B. Cunningham "to be put
to college until he obtains a degree." d. Jenny; s. John Whitfield Cun-
ningham; s. Alexander Newton Cunningham; s. William Madison
Cunningham; d. Martha Rowe Cunningham.
Teste: John Nelson, John Helm, John Jordan.
May Sessions, 1812.

P. 119—Will of Anthony McNutt:
April 10, 1818. D. Jane Russell; Alexander Ferguson, husband of
my daughter Polly. Thomas Ferguson and David Russell, Exs.

P. 120—Will of Abigail Job:
March 8, 1819. Children: Abraham Job; Sarah Humphreys, Phebe
Gibson, Joshua Job, Rebecca Carr, John Job. Son Joshua, Ex.
Teste: Isaac Little, Abraham Hoss, Elijah Broom.
April Sessions, 1819.

P. 158—Will of John Snapp, Sen'r:
Oct. 9, 1818. Wife Mary; s. John Snapp, Jun'r, S. Joseph. d. Mar-
garet Spangler; son-in-law George Houston who m. d. Susanna; "land on
Mill creek Rockingham Co., Va."
Teste: John Doan, Daniel Yeager, Robert S. Kennedy, David Wallis,
Susanna Yerger.
January Sessions, 1819.

MARRIAGE RECORDS, BLOUNT COUNTY, TENNESSEE

Alexander, Benjamin ...Ruth Wallace........Sept. 16, 1799 .Robert Hook
Alexander, William.....Ann Bigham...........Sept. 5, 1800 ....Joseph Alexander
Allin, Edwin..........Sarah Allin...........Dec. 22, 1801....Wm. Gout
Allison, Robert.......Jenny Thompson......March 22, 1802..Wm. Armstrong
Andes, John..........Seline B. Bailiss.......May 27, 1799....W. Snider
Barnes, William......Jennie Walker........Oct. 21, 1801....William Walker
Barnes, William.......Christian Bowerman....Dec. 16, 1801....Peter Bowerman
Barnes..............Betsy Walker.........March 2, 1802...John Leek
Bazel, Johnathan......Nancy Mills.........Aug. 19, 1796...Samuel Huchison
Beatie, John..........Sally Rider...........July 15, 1800....John Bradley
Bell, Burrel..........Sophia Yancey........Jan. 17, 1797 ....Austin Yancey
Bell, John...........Jane Craig...........Apr. 17, 1795 ..James Bell
Bell, John...........Nancy Weir..........Mar. 9, 1801 ....John Carson
Berry, James.........Rebecca Rogers.......Aug. 20, 1798 ...Hugh S. Cochran
Blair, William........Betsy McDowell.......Dec. 20, 1799....Henry Beard
Blevins, Richard......Elizabeth Arenton.....Nov. 5, 1800 ...Michael Holder
Bogle, Hugh.........Hannah Caldwell .....Apr. 2, 1801 ...Andrew Bogle, Sr.
Bogle, Samuel.........Nelly Williams ....Sept. 14, 1797 ..James Upton
Borden, Adam........Betsy Huchison.......Sept. 4, 1800 ....John Kee
Bowerman, Michael ...Cathy Bowers........Feb. 25, 1800...James Sloan
Boyd, James..........Hannah McMurray....Sept. 3, 1797
Boyd, James..........Ann Miller...........Feb. 15, 1797....James Sloss
Boyd, John...........Cathy Holloway......Sept. 30, 1799 ...James Sloss
Bradley, Isom.........Susanna Mattucks......May 13, 1798 ...David Hauten
Bradley, William......Mary Murphy........June 24, 1797...Thomas Murphy
Bradley, William......Polly Clampet........Oct. 20, 1802....Elijah Clampet
Brown, David........Betsy Sloan..........June 16, 1800....John McAlroy
Brown, John..........Nancy Allen.........July 30, 1801....John Bradley
Brown, William.......Polly An Moffet.......April 12, 1800...Cornelius Bogart
Broyles, George.......Catherine Vaught......June 16, 1796....Andrew Vaut
Broyles, Jacob........Mary Vaught........April 19, 1802...George Broiles
Burnett, Edward......Rachel Cheetwood.....July 2, 1801.....James Roddy
Byrd, Abraham.......Betsy Gillespie........March 20, 1799. Joseph Young
Cabe, John...........Margaret Cooper......Feb. 21, 1798....John Jackson
Caldwell, David......Molly Russell.........Jan. 21, 1795 ....Vance Russell
Caldwell, David......Elizabeth Griffin ....Oct. 25, 1800....John Ewing
Childress, John.......Mary Curtney........Nov. 8, 1796 ....Robert Rhea
Clark, John..........Letitia Sharp.........Jan. 29, 1801 ....James Gillespie
Cates, John..........Sarah Rogers.........Jan. 12, 1796 ....James Houston
Cochran, Daniel......Ellinor Moore........Mar. 1, 1796 ....John Singleton
Cochran, Hugh L......Margaret Reagan .....Sept. 4, 1797 ....George Blackburn
Cochran, Isaac........Polly Kelly..........April 10, 1799...John Cochran
Colville, Joseph.......Martha Smart........Dec. 12, 1801....Gideon Blackburn
Cooke, David.........Kity Niamon.........March 18, 1802..Abraham Philips
Cooke, James.........Margaret Gould.......Jan. 22, 1802 ....James Sloan
Copeland, David......Susannah Craig.......June 25, 1800....James Craig
Copeland, James......Ann Cameron.......Sept. 11, 1800 ...James Craig
Copeland, Joel........Rebecka Huchison......Sept. 14, 1798 ...John Huchison
Coulter, Richard......Minner Kitchin.......June 19, 1799....John Snider
Cowan, James........Margaret Montgomery .Apr. 23, 1800 ...Samuel Cowan
Cowan, John..........Rosanna Gillespie......Aug. 23, 1797 ...James Gillespie
Cowan, Robert.......Nancy Martin.........Aug. 20, 1797 ...James Houston
Craig, Alexander......Susan Logan.........May 28, 1800 ...Hugh Ferguson
Craig, William........Ester Montgomery.....July 5, 1801.... Alexander Montgomery
Culton, James.........Peggy Weir..........Jan. 20, 1801 ....Joseph Walker
Cunningham, David....Prissy Dennis.........Jan. 13, 1798 ....Miles Cunningham
Cunningham, Miles ....Mary Denny.........May 22, 1797 ...David Cunningham
Cusick, John B........Hulda Durham........Oct. 9, 1799.....William Durham
Davenport, William ...Polly Huchland........Dec. 20, 1802....Terrence Conner
Dickson, John.........Maryan Edmonson.....Oct. 30, 1802....Samuel Hendley

Doherty, George	Nancy McDowell	Apr. 7, 1799	John McDowell
Donahoo, Charles	Margaret Weir	Jan. 8, 1802	Joseph Weir
Donald, James	Elizabeth Hendricks	Sept. 9, 1796	Arch Lackey
Donald, Matthew	Agnes Walker	Dec. 9, 1802	John Cochran
Dunlap, Adam	Margery Porter	Jan. 31, 1797	Samuel Porter
Dunlap, James	Margaret Palmer	Dec. 26, 1798	Stephen Graves
Eakin, Samuel	Polly Walker	Apr. 30, 1801	Humphrey Montgom'r
Edmiston, James	Agnes Alexander	Oct. 2, 1797	James Ewing
Egleton, David	Elizabeth Hooks	Dec. 2, 1797	Alex Lackey
Ewing, James	Mary Thompson	Apr. 30, 1797	James Edmiston
Ewing, William	Elizabeth McNutt	Nov. 9, 1796	Alex McCullock
Fair, Jesse	Jenny Conaway	Oct. 13, 1801	Jesse Conoway
Fisher, John	Jean Palmer	July 25, 1800	James Craig
Falkner, Joseph	Martha Franks	July 21, 1800	James Falkner
Ferguson, Hugh	Martha Craig	Nov. 9, 1796	William Gay
Francis, William	Rebecca Miller	Oct. 19, 1801	James Danforth
Frankland, Esom	Rebecca Major	July 17, 1797	Samuel Major
Franklin, George	Jenney Shaw	Sept. 1, 1802	Josiah Payne
Frankland, John	Polly Erwin	Aug. 20, 1797	Wm. E. Erwin
Friar, John	Jobetha Avery	Nov. 11, 1799	
Fox, James N.	Prudence Felkner	Dec. 1, 1802	James Felkner
Gamble, Andrew	Elizabeth Davidson	Apr. 23, 1799	Wm. Armstrong
Gamble, Hugh	Betsy Wittenbarger	Dec. 21, 1799	Henry Whitenbarger
Gamble, John	Sarah Williams	Nov. 21, 1798	Richard Williams
Gamble, William	Sarah Gillespie	Apr. 16, 1799	Jonathan Trippet
Gammell, Wm.	Ann McGaughey	Oct. 12, 1797	Wm. Hanna
Galahar, Joseph	Margaret Gillespie	Apr. 16, 1799	John Cochran
Garner, John	Rachel Henry	Oct. 17, 1798	James Garner
Gilmore, James	Sarah Glass	Aug. 30, 1801	Alex Redford
Gilmore, John	Elenor McKinney	Mar. 13, 1797	Andrew Woods
Gilmore, Matthew	Margaret Logan	July 14, 1800	Geo. Davison
Gillespie, Alexander	Margaret Young	Aug. 3, 1799	Robert Young
Gillespie, Alexander	Sarah Rhodes	Sept. 28, 1802	Robert Bailey
Gillespie, John	Betsy Houston	Feb. 7, 1799	John Gillespie
Gillespie, John	Ann Chamberlain	Oct. 18, 1802	Wm. Gillespie
Gillespie, Zack	Elizabeth Roads	Apr. 16, 1802	Geo. Montgomery
Gold, Samuel	Mary Jackson	Sept. 17, 1797	Robert Wilson
Goodman, Amos	Sarah Conway	Aug. 30, 1801	Thos. Conway
Greer, Arthur	Jenny Hart	Aug. 29, 1799	Joseph Hart
Griffitts, Wm.	Mary Matthews	June 15, 1799	Hugh Hackney
Hackney, Hugh	Ann Lambert	June 15, 1799	Wm. Griffitts
Hamelton, Wm.	Elizabeth Rogers	Aug. 24, 1800	David Lovelace
Hamton, James	Mary Gillespie	Oct. 6, 1796	Barkley McGhee
Hail, Thomas	Rosana Denne	Apr. 23, 1801	Luke Hail
Hamontree, James	Nancy Holoway	Apr. 30, 1800	John Holloway
Hammil, John	Ann Rowan	Nov. 9, 1797	Josiah Danforth
Hanna, John	Jane Trimble	Feb. 15, 1796	Wm. Cochran
Hanna, John	Martha Miller	Sept. 5, 1796	Wm. Miller
Hanna, Joseph	Mary Walker	March 25, 1797	David Taylor
Hanna, William	Mary Moore	May 1, 1798	John Cochran
Harle, Baldwin	Isabella Miller	Feb. 13, 1800	
Harp, McAjor	Susanna Roberts	Sept. 5, 1797	John Roberts
Henry, Samuel	Elizabeth Garnor	March 26, 1798	George Colville
Henry, William	Polly Gamble	Dec. 10, 1800	Samuel Henry
Hoff, Daniel	Betsy Chisom	Jan. 9, 1798	John Chisom
Hooks, Robert	Abigail Alexander	Nov. 27, 1795	John Alexander
Howard, Ephraim	Elizabeth Vaught	June 23, 1797	Isaiah Stephens
Hughes, Moses	Miriam Kelsoe	Apr. 15, 1801	James Mayo
Hussey, Elijah	Elizabeth Baker	Jan. 25, 1801	Wm. Baker
Hutton, Josiah	Isabella McConnal	Jan. 5, 1796	James McConnal
Jackson, Andrew	Jean Sloan	June 8, 1797	Samuel Gould

Jones, Orin..........Susannah Rodgers......Nov. 24, 1802 ...John Rodgers
Jones, Samuel........Joanna Allin.........Nov. 23, 1800 ...Thomas Jones
Johnston, Francis......Polly Johnston........Nov. 23, 1802 ...David Oats
Journey, Joseph.......Elizabeth Jackson .....June 2, 1801.....Joseph Doherty
Kelly, Alex...........Black...............May 27, 1802 ...David Craig
Kelly, John..........Nancy Mayho.........Apr. 9, 1797 ...John Cochran
Kennedy, Felix.......Betsy Long.........Sept. 15, 1800 ...John Kennedy
King, John...........Becky Pride...........June 11, 1801....Samuel King
King, Samuel.........Agnes Hanna.........Aug. 26, 1797 ...Samuel Eakin
Kyle, Marion.........Betsy Posey.........Dec. 25, 1802...Isaac D. Wilson
Lackey, Andrew.......Esther Johnson........Dec. 25, 1800....Woods Lackey
Lackey, Arch.........Isabella Trimble ......Dec. 24, 1798....John Trimble
Lakes, Thos..........Jenny Majors.........Jan. 1, 1800 .....Samuel Majors
Legg, Isaac..........Mary Horsley.........Sept. 6, 1798 ....Ambrose Legg
Letherdale, Wm.......Elizabeth Willis........Mar. 16, 1799 ...James Willis
Likens, John.........Isabella Sloan.........Aug. 22, 1792 ...David Brown
Lovelace, Barton......Mary Lowe...........June 30, 1798....Wm. McNabb
Lowrey, William......Ann Wallace.........Mar. 17, 1797 ...Wm. Wallace
McCammon, John .....Elizabeth Tipton......May 14, 1798 ...James Tipton
McCandlas, James ....Elizabeth Caldwell .....Feb. 10, 1801....John Kelly
McClanahan, Mathew..Sally Bradley.........May 16, 1801 ...Robert McMurray
McClure, James.......Margaret Gamble.....Sept. 12, 1797 ...Samuel King
McCollom, John.......Elizabeth Bolton......Feb. 9, 1801....James Falkner
McCullough, Alexander Margaret McNutt.....Sept. 20, 1795 ...Wm. Ewing
McCombs, John.......Lethia Davis.........May 13, 1801....Henry Long
McConnell, James .....Ann McKee.........Aug. 26, 1800 ...Andrew Gamill
McCulloch, Sam.......Peggy Porter.........Oct. 22, 1800....James McCulloch
McCord, James........Dorcas Cowan........May 30, 1801 ...Samuel Handley
McCoughorne, John....Hannah Johnston......March 18, 1802..Robert Pearce
McDowell, James......Nancy Conner........Sept. 30, 1799 ...James McLanahan
McDowel, John.......Pheby Frankland......Sept. 20, 1797 ...Francis Irwin
McGaughey, James.....Margaret McCain .....Apr. 12, 1798 ...Wm. McGaughey
McGuire, Isaac........Martha Jackson........July 14, 1796....John Dinning
McKenzey, Daniel .....Jennie Tippett........Dec. 20, 1798...James Mitchell
McReynolds, John......Jane McReynolds......Nov. 27, 1799 ...Joseph Alexander
McTeer, James........Martha Ferguson......Sept. 29, 1795....Barkley McGhee
McTeer, James........Jenny McTeer.........Aug. 7, 1798 ....Wm. Glass
McTeer, Robert.......Mary Sherrall.........March 22, 1798..John McTeer
McTeer, William......Mary McTeer.........Oct. 20, 1802....Jacob Moore
Mathew, Jonathan.....Mary Allin...........Nov. 23, 1800 ...Thomas Jones
Maxwell, James.......Mary Majors.........May 22, 1802 ...John Murphy
Maxwell, James.......Sarah Moore.........Aug. 18, 1802 ...John Gillespie
Maxwell, Thomas......Esther Hogg.........Sept. 17, 1798 ...John Simmons
May, James...........................Feb. 16, 1801................
Meeks, Jeremiah.......Betsy Blevins.........Feb. 8, 1802.....John Kee
Miller, Cullinus ......Polly Sloan ....Oct. 22, 1800....James Boyd
Miller, John..........Sally Wood...........Aug. 5, 1801 ....Thomas Taylor
Montgomery, David....Margaret McCollum ...Feb. 7, 1799....Matthew Wallace
Montgomery, James....Charity Garritson......Sept. 9, 1802 ....Andrew Agnew
Montgomery, John.....Peggy Alexander.......Nov. 23, 1798 ...George Wallace
Montgomery, John.....Patsey Machesney ....June 9, 1801.....Thomas Berry
Moore, Willis.........Mary Clampet........Oct. 20, 1795....John Cochran
Moore, Wm., Jr........Jenny Montgomery ....May 5, 1802 ....Hugh Montgomery
Morrison, Thomas .....Frances Beard.........Aug. 23, 1799 ...George Beard
Mickle (Eickle), John ...Rebecca Hussey ......June 12, 1801....Elijah Brown
Neily, Wm............Jane Hogg...........Feb. 6, 1800.....Soloman McCampbell
Netherton, John........Elizabeth Harden......Aug. 9, 1797 ...A. Rogan
Nickel, William.......Elizabeth Vaune.......Aug. 19, 1796 ...John Trimble
Penter, John..........Sarah Waters.........June 26, 1802....Thomas Clark
Parkhill, David........Martha Wosham.......Aug. 2, 1799 ....John Trimble
Pinexo, Francisco .....Liddy Casteel.........Mar. 5, 1800 ....Joseph Casteel

Rankin, John . . . . Peggy Wier . . . . Feb. 23, 1801 . . . . Absolem Wilson
Ray, Jesse . . . . Margaret Blair . . . . Dec. 7, 1802 . . . . . Wm. Blair
Rhea, John . . . . Rebecca Miller . . . . Mar. 3, 1800 . . . . James Rhea
Richardson, Edward . . . . Sarah Reed . . . . Mar. 31, 1798 . . . James Blair
Ritchie, Thomas . . . . . . Jenny Gannaway . . . . . . May 25, 1800 . . . . John Trimble
Roberts, John . . . . Rachel Robenett . . . . . . Dec. 9, 1796 . . . . Jacob Meek
Roberts, Peter . . . . Mary Blevins . . . . Mar. 9, 1801 . . . John Key
Rogers, James . . . . Anna Blair . . . . Mar. 12, 1800 . . . Isaiah Brown
Rogers, Thomas . . . . . . Mary W. Carter . . . . . . July 5, 1796 . . . . John Hickley
Rowan, Samuel . . . . Jean Cowan . . . . Aug. 7, 1798 . . . Samuel Gould
Russell, Hance . . . . Elizabeth McClannahan Sept. 21, 1796 . . James Gannaway
Russell, James . . . . Mary Hitchcock . . . . . . Aug. 3, 1802 . . . John Russell
Russell, John . . . . Jenny McNutt . . . . March 2, 1801 . . Edward Sharp
Shields, Branner . . . . . . Peggy Weir . . . . Feb. 5, 1800 . . . . . Jonathan Trippett
Simpson, Wm. . . . . Sarah Beaty . . . . Sept. 21, 1801 . . . John Beaty
Sanders, John . . . . Silvia Baless . . . . May 27, 1799
Shankland, John . . . . . . Lidda Hart . . . . June 14, 1796 . . . Joseph Hart
Sloan, Robert . . . . Peggy Cooke . . . . Dec. 26, 1801 . . . David Cooke
Smith, John . . . . Sarah Caceper . . . . May 2, 1801 . . . . George Townsley
Spilman, Thomas . . . . . . Charity Jones . . . . July 24, 1798 . . . Lewis Jones
Stigall, Benjamin . . . . . . Patsey Denney . . . . Aug. 20, 1802 . . . Joseph Thurman
Stephens, John . . . . Rebecca Clampet . . . . . . Oct. 24, 1797 . . . Norton Green
Stockton, Marshel . . . . . Mary Kindreck . . . . Feb. 4, 1801 . . . . David Lovelace
Stewart, Robert . . . . . . Elizabeth Stevenson . . . Dec. 22, 1800 . . . Elijah Stevenson
Teague, Magness . . . . . Frances Rodgers . . . . . Jan. 2, 1798 . . . . . John Rodgers
Tebbs, John . . . . Mary More . . . . Dec. 30, 1799 . . . Thomas Rodgers
Tedford, John . . . . Jean Henderson . . . . Dec. 11, 1799 . . . George Tedford
Tedford, Robert . . . . . . Jenny White . . . . July 4, 1800 . . . . . John Craig
Tedford, Thomas . . . . . Polly Hannah . . . . Oct. 21, 1800 . . . Robert Hannah
Terry, Samuel . . . . Sarah Hail . . . . Oct. 3, 1797 . . . . . Daniel Hoff
Thompson, James . . . . . Susannah Weir . . . . June 30, 1797 . . . John Weir
Thompson, John . . . . . . Margaret McConald . . . May 30, 1799 . . Samuel Cowan
Timberman, Abraham . . Nancy Hawkins . . . . Jan. 19, 1801 . . . . Christopher Timberman
Timberman, Christopher Mary Ferguson . . . . Oct. 14, 1800 . . . Jona. Timmerman
Tipton, Benjamin . . . . . . Rebecca Cusic . . . . Dec. 19, 1796 . . . Robert Hooks
Tipton, James . . . . Agness Leions . . . . Apr. 7, 1800 . . . . James Gillespie
Tipton, William . . . . . . Peggy Tipton . . . . Jan. 22, 1802 . . . John Tipton
                                                             Andrew Thompson
Trice, John . . . . Tabitha Ewing . . . . Nov. 11, 1799 . . . Henry Beazel
Vaut, Andrew . . . . Susanna Broils . . . . Dec. 16, 1800 . . . Stephen Boutwell
Walker, Hugh . . . . Nancy Cochran . . . . June 5, 1797 . . . . Hugh L. Cochran, Sr.
Walker, Samuel . . . . Rebecca Davidson . . . . March 20, 1802 . . John Walker
Wallace, Abraham . . . . Sept. 9, 1802 . . . . William Lowrey
Wallace, David . . . . Sarah Justice . . . . April 23, 1798 . . Moses Justice
Wallace, James . . . . Sarah Runnils . . . . Dec. 31, 1801 . . . William Wallace
Wallace, Jesse . . . . Margaret Gow . . . . Sept. 7, 1801 . . . Erastus Tippet
Wallace, John . . . . Jean Blackburn . . . . May 22, 1798 . . . John Cowan
Washbutn, Sherod . . . . . Mary Hutson . . . . Jan. 26, 1800 . . . Andrew Richey
Watson . . . . Nave . . . . Oct. 1, 1801 . . . . . George Nave
Wear, Samuel . . . . Polly Gallaher . . . . Sept. 30, 1799 . . . Jacob Johnson
Weir, Hugh . . . . Jean Weir . . . . Jan. 20, 1801 . . . . James Weir
Weir, James . . . . Martha (Patsey) Rankin July 22, 1802 . . . John Waugh
Weir, John . . . . Jenny Weir . . . . June 3, 1797 . . . . . William Beard
Williams, Henry . . . . . . Bethsheba Jones . . . . . . July 13, 1802 . . . David Oatts
Williams, John . . . . Agness Bogle . . . . Sept. 7, 1797 . . . Samuel Bogle
Williams, Richard . . . . . Sally Williams . . . . July 25, 1800 . . . Samuel Bogle
Willis, Jacob . . . . Margaret Majors . . . . . . Aug. 20, 1798 . . . Armstead Thornhill
Wilson, Hugh . . . . Susy Shields . . . . Feb. 10, 1801 . . . George Shiels
Wilson, James . . . . Elizabeth Weir . . . . Nov. 10, 1802 . . . Josiah Payne
Woods, Patrick . . . . Jenny Hanna . . . . June 12, 1799 . . . Robert Hanna
Wosham, Jeremiah . . . . Jean King . . . . Sept. 18, 1802 . . . Thomas Simpson

MARRIAGE RECORDS, DAVIDSON COUNTY, TENNESSEE
MARRIAGE REGISTER, VOLUME I

P. 1: William Haythorn to Mary Kelley. Jan. 11, 1793.
Nehemiah Courtney to Elizabeth Johnston. Oct. 14, 1790.
Andrew Buchanon to Jane McKiney. Oct. 22, 1798.
Amos Rounswall to Elizabeth Thomas. Sept. 10, 1794.
James Rutherford to Elizabeth Cartwright. Jan. 7, 1791.
John Dunham to Polly Waller. Nov. 2, 1793.
Wm. Flynn to Hannah Ramsey. May 8, 1793.
Jacob Crow to Nancy Crow. July 5, 1793.
Bosley Beal to Margery Shute. Dec. 24, 1794.

P. 2: Thomas Heaton to Mary Stuart. July 19, 1794.
Benj. Downey to Mary Hollis. March 22, 1794.
James Dean to Polly Dickinson. Sept. 24, 1794.
Wm. Bodie to Jennie Lane. June 19, 1790.
George Walker to Rachel Caffrey. Aug. 9, 1790.
Chas. Snyder to Elizabeth Savier. —— 18, 1790.
Cornelius Glasgow to Lucia Merida. Nov. 15, 1793.
Finis Ewing to Peggy Davidson. Jan. 12, 1793.
Thomas Wilcocks to Mary Bryant. Sept. 12, 1792.
Thomas Brown to Mary Love. June 27, 1791.

P. 3: John Champ to Polly Mayfield. Dec. 21, 1796.
Wm. Neely to Hennie Buchanan. Apr. 20, 1791.
Jacob Reader to Polly Allen. July 2, 1792.
Wm. Hooper to Sarah Hollis. March 4, 1789.
Seward Slayton to Nancy Williams. July 8, 1789.
Jacob Guise to Elizabeth Bigley. Feb. 2, 1789.
Joshua Harlin to Mary Smith. Nov. 17, 1789.
John Kirkpatrick to Martha Buchanan. Sept. 6, 1789.
Robert Nelson to Elizabeth Bell. Sept. 1, 1789.

P. 4: Joshua Hollis to Mary Wilheim. Aug. 19, 1789.
Josiah Payne to Mary Barnett. May 4, 1789.
Robert Mitchell to Duijila Everett. June 1, 1789.
Abijah Harrington to Sarah Marrs. Nov. 19, 1789.
Robert Barnett to Margaret Young. July 31, 1789.
Simon Rogers to Elizabeth Mitchell. March 7, 1789.
Wm. Hudson to Elizabeth Dunn. Oct. 15, 1789.
Francis Rordin to Rebecca Cashard. March 9, 1790.
Wm. Murry to Margaret Boyd. March 31, 1790.
Mitchell O'neal to Delilah Martin. March 5, 1790.

P. 5: Richard Hightower to Nancy Smith.   Oct. 17, 1791.
       Ralph Flemming to Hannah Boyd.   Apr. 13, 1791.
       Elisha Brewer to Mary Renolds.   May 17, 1791.
       James Whitsett to Jennie Meneso.   Dec. 10, 1792.
       Henry Green to Jennie Davidson.   July 4, 1791.
       Peter Caffrey to ———— ————.   Jan. 5, 1791.
       Joseph Dunham to Nancy Bronson.   Nov. 24, 1793.
       Mitchell O'neal to Judith Hughes.   March 19, 1793.
       Henry Chiles to Sally Suggs.   Sept. 11, 1793.
       John Wilson to Nancy McNight.   Sept. 10, 1791

P. 6: Ephraim Pratt to Sarah Buchanan.   June 28, 1790.
       David Shaffer to Jane Bowlin.   Jan. 23, 1792.
       Joseph Hart to Anna Suggs.   Aug. 21, 1791.
       Michael Black to Eva Raimer.   Oct. 3, 1791.
       Richard Shaffer to Elizabeth Gambul.   Oct. 21, 1789.
       Philip Pipkin to Margaret Brown.   ———— 8, 1792.
       Witherel Latimer to Margaret Anderson.   March 21, 1793.
       Matthew McCance to Anna Walker.   March 24, 1794.
       Andrew Jackson to Rachel Donelson.   Jan. 17, 1794.

P. 7: Zacheus Baker to Elsee Rhods.   Oct. 24, 1794.
       Abraham Boyd to Nancy Lyon.   April 1, 1794.
       William McClish to Jennie Johnston.   Nov. 10, 1794.
       Michael Squires to Martha Turner.   July 7, 1792.
       Charles Campbell to Ann Nowland.   May 4, 1791.
       Wm. Smith to Phoebe Denton.   September 4, 1792.
       Lewis Berryal to Jean Benton.   ————
       Daniel Evans to Elizabeth Courtney.   Feb. 8, 1794.
       William Moore to Palifina Castleman.   Dec. 7, 1791.
       John Buchanan to Hannah Buchanan.   June 6, 1794.

P. 8: Adam Raimer to Mary Carihan.   May 30, 1791.
       John Topp to Comfort Everett.   July 26, 1794.
       Wm. Murry, Elizabeth Pillow.   July 16, 1795.
       Jacob Edwards to Elizabeth Hale.   April 3, 1795.
       James Bleakley to Nancy Wilkison.   December 19, 1795.
       James Robertson to Mary Bradshaw.   December 15, 1795.
       Robert Rosebury to Susannah McGaugh.   Jan. 3, 1795.
       John Alston to Sinah Hooper.   June 3, 1795.
       Wm. Payne to Elizabeth Payne. June 10, 1796.
       Elijah Hixon to Polly Moore.   August 22, 1796.

P. 9:   David Young to Sarah Philips.   Dec. 27, 1796.
        John Evans to Polly Thomas.   Aug. 24, 1796.
        Wm. Donelson to Charity Dickinson.   Aug. 9, 1796.
        Daniel Helton to Elizabeth Lancaster.   July 26, 1796.
        W. Dillahunty to Sarah Johnson.   Oct. 10, 1796.
        Hugh Perry to Jane Kendrick.   Nov. 4, 1796.
        Joseph Walker to Sarah Carothers.   Jan. 18, 1796.
        John Witherspoon to Elizabeth Shute.   Jan. 31, 1796.
        John Shute to Nancy Childress.   Dec. 5, 1796.
        John Harris to Eliza Lucas.   Jan. 20, 1796.

P. 10: Joseph Ralston to Jane Walker.   April 25, 1796.
        Frederick Ward to Mary Bosley.   May 26, 1796.
        Holland Darden to Charlotte Crawford.   Nov. 14, 1796.
        Thomas Buchanan to Jenny Neely.   June 6, 1796.
        Eneas Hooper to Anne Young.   March 10, 1796.
        Joseph Brown to Sarah Thomas.   ——— 18, 1796.
        Samuel McBride to Elizabeth Howell.   January 4, 1796.
        Barnabeth Harrod to Polly Williams.   May 4, 1795.
        Jeremiah Loftin to Hanna Dillihunt.   June 4, 1796.

P. 11: Noel Watkins to Sallie Smith.   Sept. 11, 1797.
        David Walker to Phoebe Finley.   Sept. 25, 1797.
        Daniel Small to Mary Hutchens.   Nov. 27, 1797.
        James Hodge to Nancy Becton.   Jan. 25, 1797.
        James Stuart to Sally Hooper.   Feb. 4, 1797.
        Joshua Balance to Mary D. Roberts.   Oct. 10, 1797.
        Moses Smith to Ruth Smith.   Dec. 30, 1797.
        Jesse Thomas to Mary Drucilla Tracey.   Dec. 1, 1797.
        Joel Parish to Hannah Smith.   Dec. 3, 1797.
        Anthony Hampton to Polly Williams.   Dec. 20, 1797.

P. 12: Pleasant McQuerry to Nancy Smith.   Sept. 27, 1797.
        Baldwin Huddleston to Rebecca Henderson.   June 14, 1797.
        Daniel Miles to Susanna Frensley.   Oct. 17, 1797.
        Thomas Lancaster to Anna Walker.   Dec. 13, 1797.
        Robert Smith to Mary T. Donelson.   Nov. 30, 1798.
        Abraham Walker to Martha Patten.   March 31, 1798.
        John McAllister to Mary N. Bearding.   March 9, 1789.
        James Fairless to Mary Armstrong.   Jan. 4, 1798.
        Permot Wiggin to Rachel Wendle.   March 9, 1798.
        James Hill to Mary S. Hunt.   Dec. 18, 1798.

P. 13: William Mullen to Mary S. Becton.   Nov. 29, 1798.
      Alexander Moore to Mary Cloyd.   Feb. 22, 1798.
      Henry Phenix to Nancy Todd.   Feb. 11, 1798.
      David Castleman to Mary Campbell.   March 22, 1798.
      Jeremiah Fly to Mary Z. Pimpkins.   Jan. 16, 1798.
      Thomas Rutherford to Mary Woodard.   Jan. 18, 1799.
      Daniel Ross to Martha C. Napier.   Jan. 12, 1799.
      Wm. Smith to Polly Heaton.   Jan. 9, 1798.
      John Campbell to Nettie Boren.   Oct. 10, 1799.

P. 14: John Walker to Maria Enochs.   Jan. 12, 1803.
      Benjamin Thomas to Mary Amelia Thomas.   Sept. 23, 1800.
      James Reaves to Polly Gower.   July 8, 1800.
      Richard Clark to Elizabeth Farman.   March 23, 1796.
      Harris Dowlin to Susannah Hargrave.   ———— 16, 1799.
      Abraham Nolen to Elizabeth Blithe.   May 5, 1797.
      John Long to Winnie Watts.   Jan. 7, 1797.
      Isom S. Parker to Peggy Curtis.   March 27, 1797.
      Hugh Allison to Lidia Harrison.   March 24, 1797.
      John Miller to Prudence Gower.   March 20, 1797.

P. 15: Roberto Smith to Martha McNight.   Oct. 14, 1797.
      Alexander Chambers to Darky Tracy.   March 25, 1797.
      Bennet Search to Nancy Croww.   Dec. 17, 1796.
      Henry Wegh to Ruth Logne (no date—in 1796 file).
      Cornelius Anderson to Mary Scott.   Dec. 2, 1796.
      James Neely to Helly Philips (Supposed 1796.)
      James Thomas to Elizabeth Duke.   April 15, 1797.
      George Shannon to Mary McNight.   May 2, 1797.
      Alexander Bingham to Winefred Reeves.   Feb. 2, 1797.
      Thomas Gleaves to Sallie Smith.   March 13, 1797.

P. 16: Joseph Johnston to Rachel Dillahunty.   Sept. 1, 1796.
      John Johnson to Isabell Reaves.   April 29, 1797.
      Sam McNight to Sally Smith.   Feb. 28 (Supposed 1796).
      Isaac Weakley to Sarah McGaugh.   March 10, 1797.
      John Porter to Lucy Hopkins.   Jan. 7, 1797.
      David Koen to Patsey Winstead.   Sept. 21, 1800.
      Joseph T. Elliston to Louisa Mullen.   Aug. 20, 1800.
      Smith Felen to Sallie Webb.   June 28, 1800.
      Frederich Oliver to Rosanna Oliver.   July 6, 1800.
      Wm. Chapman to Sallie Oglesby.   June 26, 1800.

P. 17   Jonathan Brady to Elizabeth Hanes. June 28, 1800.
      Joshua Tarkington to Polly Berry. Sept. 15, 1800.
      Claiborne Williams to Miss Shumate. Sept. 25, 1800.
      Allen Mathes to Lenora Perry. Oct. 27, 1800.
      Ben Whitehead to Sallie Hargrove. Sept. 16, 1800.
      Thomas Laremore to Elizabeth Atkins. Aug. 9, 1800.
      Marvel Low. Mary Harris. Aug. 25, 1800.
      John Fielder to Mary J. McCutcheon. July 19, 1800.
      Elisha Bellemmy to Hannah Standsberry. Oct. 28, 1800.
      Simeon Morriss to Nancy Haile. Dec. 9, 1800.

P. 18   James McAlister to Jennie Mills. July 19, 1800.
      John Sharlock to Mary J. Williamson. Sept. 22, 1800.
      Eleazer Hardeman to Elizabeth Foster. Aug. 20, 1800.
      Samuel Stockell to Bettie Johnston. Aug. 16, 1800.
      Joseph Edwards to Patsy Rodgers. Sept. 2, 1800.
      William Smith to Nancy Powell. Jan. 20, 1801.
      Nicholas Crossy to Ann Cole. July 4, 1801.
      Charles Lynn to Nancy Payne. June 15, 1801.
      Enoch Dauge to Margaret Average. March 4, 1801.
      William Shute to Olive Collingsworth. Jan. 7, 1801.

P. 19   John Jacbson to Jovis Kren. Feb. 21, 1801.
      John Shouse to Sallie Collins. May 4, 1801.
      Daniel Koen to Rachel Jackson. Sept. 16, 1801.
      Richard Williams to Tabitha Topp. Jan. 27, 1801.
      Samuel Koen to Lelia Hooper. Feb. 21, 1801.
      Thomas A. Claiborne to Sarah T. Lewis. April 20, 1801.
      John Bowers to Elizabeth Foster. Jan. 7, 1801.
      Wm. Parker to Sallie Littleton. July 14, 1801.
      Abraham Green to Patsy Caffrey. Jan. 7, 1801.
      Philemon Duke to Sallie Heaton. June 9, 1801.

P. 20   Thomas Lightfoot to Sallie Allen. April 10, 1801.
      Charles Simmons to Polly Thompson. April 15, 1801.
      Joseph Buckler to Elizabeth Hampton. Sept. 15, 1801.
      Thomas Simpson to Drucilla Verra. April 6, 1801.
      John Thomas to Sallie Eatherly. Feb. 7, 1801.
      David Lunn to Nancy Leek. May 9, 1801.
      Spirus Roach to Margaret Curry. June 30, 1801.
      George Bradberry to Mary Taylor. April 21, 1801.
      James Gulleford to Susannah Eatherly. Feb. 27, 1801.
      Sion Hunt to Rebecca Dunham. Feb. 11, 1801.

P. 21 Isaac Daws to Nancy Quilling.   April 29, 1801.
Mark Noble to Anne Jackson.   Feb. 28, 1801.
Benj. Ratcliff to Anna Davis.   Dec. 29, 1804.
Richard Boyd to Rachel Horton.   Nov. 22, 1804.
Alexander W. Stephenson to Patty Robertson.   Feb. 7, 1805.
John Buchanan to Peggy Sample.   Sept. 18, 1805.
James Brown to Polly Lucas.   Dec. 27, 1805.
Wm. Hemphill (no name given).   Feb. 13, 1805.
Wm. R. Miller to Elizabeth Overall.   Dec. 13, 1805.
John L. Young to Nancy Boyd.   April 12, 1805.
(Ed. Note—pp. 22 to 25 run through 1806.)

P. 26 Thomas Murrey to Hannah Bushart.   Oct. 12, 1790.
John Tilly to Jennie Blair.   Nov. 1791.
Kennedy Bay to Jennie Reed.   March 22, 1791.
Henry McLaughlin to Ann Harkin.   Dec. 3, 1791.
Elisha Rece to Anna Collier.   May 20, 1791.
John Billingsley to Martha Blair.   Aug. 14, 1792.
Matthew Payne to Amelia Cooper.   June 17, 1791.
Joseph Shannon to Mary Billingsley.   Nov. 24, 1792.
Mitchel O'Neal to Judith Hughes.   March 18, 1793.
Joseph Desaque to Elizabeth Bennett.   March 12, 1793.

P. 27 Peter B. Stuart to Senath Lucas.   July 24, 1793.
James Brient to Mary Lee.   June 17, 1793.
William Neely to Esther Walker.   March 18, 1793.
John Anderson to Hannah Sutton.   May 29, 1793.
Joseph Porter to Elizabeth Thomas.   July 21st, 1794.
James Collinsworth to Jennie Brown.   July 26, 1794.
Henry Lane to Margaret Moore.   July 28, 1794.
Reubin Parkes to Charity Johnston.   Jan. 20, 1794.
Nicholas Boeter to Nancy Johnston.   January 2, 1794.
John Perry to Charity Baker.   Jan. 7, 1794.

P. 28 Thomas Gorham to Sallie W. Suggs.   Oct. 5, 1795.
Henry Skinner to Jane Hays.   Jan. 11, 1792.
Richard Lancaster to Jane Vernon.   April 25, 1795.
Malachiah Sutton to Hannah Moore.   Sept. 13, 1792.
John Carpenter to Mary Fisher.   Dec. 18, 1795.
William Ervin to Nancy Lucas.   Jan. 26, 1795.
John Edmonson to Mary Buchanan.   Sept. 6, 1796.
John Kennedy to Louisa Simpson.   Aug. 6, 1796.
William Gowen to Martha Rains.   Dec. 3, 1797.

P. 29   John McGough to Nancy Parker.   June 26, 1793.
Matthew Hunt to Nancy Kimbro.   Nov. 13, 1797.
Stephen O'Dair to Susannah Thomas.   July 26, 1797.
John McNight to Patsy Hughes.   Sept. 27, 1797.
Jeremiah Hinton to Sarah Boyd.   Oct. 18, 1797.
Josiah Sugg to Elizabeth Johns.   Aug. 14, 1797.
Wene Beardin to Mary McAlister.   Dec. 30, 1797.
Charles Hays to Anna Blackman.   June 17, 1797.
Robert Evans to Betsy Robertson.   Sept. 21, 1797.
James Olifant to Polly Compton.   Sept. 1, 1797.

P. 30   Wm. Gullage to Tempe Jones.   Dec. 22, 1797.
Tobias Adams to Isabella Gibson.   Jan. 7, 1791.
Deliverance Gray to Palmer Halstead.   June 29, 1791.
Samuel Bell to Margaret Edmondson.   June 14, 1791.
Squire Choat to Rebecca Smith.   Sept. 11, 1792.
James Robertson to Sally Ridley.   May 5, 1792.
Samuel McCutchen to Cathrine Bell.   Aug. 6, 1791.
John Buchanan to Jane Patterson.   Dec. 31, 1792.
John J. Morris to Sarah Shoat.   April 5, 1792.

P. 31   James Everett to Lettie Ridley.   May 5, 1792.
Richard Frenleyson to Elizabeth Black.   May 18, 1793.
Hi Turney to Martha Lancaster.   Dec. 13, 1788.
Jeremiah Moore to Nancy Slaton.   May 30, 1796.
John L. Mishler to Mary Cassellman.   Dec. 17, 1791.
John Hamilton to Sarah Lucas.   April 10, 1794.
Amos Moore to Margaret Neely.   Sept. 17, 1791.
James McCutchen to Elizabeth Dean.   April 23, 1792.
George McLane to Parmelia Davidson.   July 20, 1789.
Patrick McCutchen to Hannah Marshall.   March 24, 1789.

P. 32   Robert White to Nancy Hays.   January 7, 1789.
William Ray to Mary MeeNees.   July 20, 1791.
William Nash to Polly Evans.   June 5, 1790.
Elijah Gowers to Prudence Coon.   Dec. 22, 1790.
David Smith to Beauty Fort.   ———— 1791.
Aquilla Carmack to Eunice Williams.   June 25, 1791.
Samuel Edmiston to Nellie Dean.   March 23, 1791.
Luke Anderson to Elizabeth Shaffer.   Aug. 1, 1794.
Evan Tracy to ———— Taylor.   August 6, 1794.
Henry Robertson to Margaret Bradhsaw.   April 3, 1793.

P. 33 William Rains to Drucilla Pillow. Sept. 9, 1795.
Oliver Williams to Betsy Hickman. Dec. 16, 1795.
James Titus to Rebecca Buchanan. June 10, 1795.
John Estes to Lenora Bayles. Sept. 15, 1795.
Isom Rogers to Margaret Mitchell. July 5, 1795.
John Castilo to Elenor Low. Aug. 3, 1795.
Robert Bell to Gazzel McCucheon. April 29, 1794.
Samuel Donelson to Mary Smith. June 30, 1796.
Ichabod Osborn to Sarah Graham. June 28, 1796.
Allison Edney to Polly Dunham. Oct. 26, 1791.

P. 34 Henry Starr to Elizabeth Chisom. March 12, 1796.
Henry Woodward to Mary Wilson. Feb. 13, 1796.
John Mitchell to Sarah Watts. Feb. 3, 1796.
Adam B. Hudson to Prissie Thomas. Oct. 11, 1797.
John Patterson to Eleanor Wilson. Dec. 27, 1797.
William Hogatt to Mary Bell. May 26, 1798.
James Dupree to Nancy Nichols. Dec. 12, 1798.
John Walker to Hepsee Hudson. Nov. 20, 1798.
Pitt Woodard to Elizabeth Smith. Nov. 16, 1795.
Moses McAfee to Sarah Chamberlin. Nov. 23, 1798.

P. 35 Joseph Malugent to Polly Mitchell. Nov. 28, 1798.
William Malugent to Polly Gee. July 25, 1798.
John Gambull to Sarah Kimbro. Nov. 1, 1798.
John Davis to Mary B. Gleaves. Aug. 4, 1798.
Richard Gatlin to Susanna Gatlin. April 12, 1798.
Aquilla Jones to Lettie Cooke. April 16, 1798.
Francis Armstrong to Elizabeth Jones. July 9, 1798.
John McKinney, Jr., to Elizabeth Buchanan. Oct. 29, 1798.
James Higdon to Sallie Thomas. July 9, 1798.
Richard Harris to Clary Elliott. July 7, 1798.

P. 36 William Fowler to Debora Liles. Oct., 1798.
Thomas Harmon to Elizabeth White. April 29, 1798.
John Garner to Margaret Carothers. Dec. 30, 1798.
John Crawford to Margaret Buchanan. Aug., 1798.
Robert Brown to Jane Robertson. Dec. 24, 1798.
Wm. McClure to Polly Lynn. Dec. 25, 1798.
Bennett Searcy to Polly Wendel. Aug. 29, 1798.
John Boyd to Elizabeth Daley. May 24, 1798.
Josiah G. Duke to Sallie Hargrove. Sept. 21, 1798.
Hartwell Miles to Polly Pillow. May 13, 1798.

P. 37　Frederick Lassiter to Rachel Rhodes.　Nov. 23, 1798.
　　　James White to Polly Gardner.　April 28, 1798.
　　　Jacob Woodrum to Jane Williamson.　Dec. 11, 1798.
　　　Alexander Smith to Sallie Leiper.　Nov. 21, 1798.
　　　George W. Lisle to Sallie Eavans.　Dec. 12, 1798.
　　　Stuart Farmbaugh to Susanna Topp.　May 21, 1798.
　　　Benjamin Drew to Nancy Buchanan.　Jan. 14, 1799.
　　　James Cummins to Elenor Waller.　Jan. 13, 1799.
　　　John Everett to Sallie Davis.　Jan. 19, 1799
　　　Isaac Berry to Polly Johnston.　Jan. 13, 1803.

P. 38　John Gregory to Susannah Corbett.　Dec. 23, 1801.
　　　John Gowen to Lydia Shute.　Oct. 30, 1801.
　　　Gabriel Joslin to Elizabeth Hooper.　Dec. 18, 1801.
　　　Henry Buford to Margaret Branch.　Dec. 12, 1801.
　　　William Curtis to Polly Drake.　Dec. 16, 1801.
　　　Robert Magness to Lydia Gamble.　Oct. 20, 1801.
　　　George G. Peyton to Frances Morris.　May 28, 1801.
　　　Joseph Gouree to Ann McSpadden.　Dec. 16, 1801.
　　　David Robertson to Elizabeth Hooper.　Dec. 19, 1801.
　　　Aaron Gamble to Elizabeth Kennedy.　Nov. 27, 1801.

P. 39　Henry M. Truett to Sally Clampett.　Dec. 13, 1801.
　　　Micajah Duke to Ann Brooks.　Dec. 2, 1801.
　　　Philip Wolf to Elizabeth Barnes.　Dec. 29, 1801.
　　　Samuel Copeland to Polly White.　Dec. 29, 1801.
　　　Joseph Pinkley to Catherine Carpenter.　June 2, 1800.
　　　John Stump to Rebecca Hyde.　May 16, 1801.
　　　Isaac Patton to Phoebe Thomas.　Oct. 5, 1801.
　　　Malachi Liles to Betsy Parker.　April 10, 1801.
　　　Joseph Caldwell Sidney Becton.　Dec. 23, 1801.
　　　M. C. Dunn to Elizabeth Rains.　Sept. 26, 1801.

P. 40　Thomas Seuder to Elizabeth Balim.　Jan. 1, 1801.
　　　Hardin Billens to Katy Hargrove.　Oct. 28, 1801.
　　　John Allsup to Sallie Robertson.　July 1, 1802.
　　　John Payne to Polly Cane.　Aug. 5, 1802.
　　　Matthew Morris to Hannah Lucas.　July 8, 1802.
　　　John Burnham to Betsy Jackson.　Aug. 28, 1802.
　　　James King to Sallie Lewis.　July 14, 1802.
　　　Ennis Hooper to Elizabeth Thomas.　Aug. 30, 1802.
　　　Leonard Keeling to Patsy Sugg.　Dec. 23, 1802.
　　　William Wilson to Sally Patterson.　Dec. 18, 1802.

REVOLUTIONARY GRANTS IN DAVIDSON COUNTY, TENNESSEE

EDITOR'S NOTE:—The following items were taken from Book One, Wills and Inventories of Davidson County.

This appears to be a general court record book, and is in the County Court Clerk's office, Nashville, Tennessee.

WILLS AND INVENTORIES—DAVIDSON COUNTY

Book 1, p. 99.

"Received of Major Mountflorence, the following warrants with the locations therein inclosed.　To Wit:

No. 293, Major Thomas Hogg—4800 acres.
No. 294, Capt. John Inglor—3840 acres.
No. 295, Capt. John Davis—3840 acres.
No. 296, Capt. Jesse Reed—3840 acres.
No. 297, Capt. William Goodman—3840 acres.
No. 298, Lieut. John Fordd—2560 acres.
No. 299, Lieut. Thos. Parteur—2560 acres.
No. 300, Private Jacob Matthews—640 acres.
No. 304, Private Theophilus Hays—640 acres.
No. 321, Private John Jeffery—640 acres.
No. 322, Private Wm. Sweet—640 acres.
No. 324, Brigade Gen'. Hogan—12,000 acres.
No. 325, Private Sam'l Garner—640 acres.
No. 326, Private Moore Walker—640 acres.
No. 327, Private Joseph Hartly—640 acres.
No. 328, Fifer Thomas Bryant—595 acres.
No. 329, Capt. John Vance—3840 acres.
No. 330, Lieut. John Vance—2560 acres.
No. 332, Maj. Wm. Fenner—2057 acres.
No. 333, Capt. Robert Fenner—3840 acres.
No. 334, Lieut. Jas. Campen—2560 acres.
No. 336, Capt. Jno. McNees—3840 acres.
No. 337, Capt. And'w Armstrong—1286 acres.
No. 339, Surgeon David Love—2057 acres.
No. 340, Capt. John Montfort—3840 acres.
No. 341, Capt. Howell Tatum—3840 acres.
No. 342, Lieut. Bount Whitmell—820 acres.
No. 345, Lieut. Anthony Crucher—2563 acres.

And on the back side of the paper was written thus: "The within mentioned warrants was Rec'd and came to hand about the 20th of December 1783 with the locations enclosed." Signed "Martin Armstrong."

Underneath:
"CAPT. ANTHONY CRUTCHER:

"Major Mountflorence informs me that the within warrants with their locations are entered in the office which must have been long after I received them as no office was established in the year eighty three but its my opinion that every of the Returns made on Such Locations Should in Justice bear date from the date Mentioned in the above Receipt To Wit. December 20th, 1783.

"Signed MARTIN ARMSTRONG."

"Teste:
    "CHARLES GARRARD."

"The last above mentioned was proven to be the Act and Deed of the sd. Armstrong by the oath of Charles Garrard in court held for the County of Davidson July term, 1789.

"Test ANDREW EWING, C. D. C."

www.ingramcontent.com/pod-product-compliance
Lightning Source LLC
Chambersburg PA
CBHW030302030426
42336CB00009B/492